BASIC CHRISTIAN LEADERSHIP

Biblical Models of Church,
Gospel and Ministry

John Stott

IVP Books
An imprint of InterVarsity Press
Downers Grove, Illinois

InterVarsity Press
P.O. Box 1400, Downers Grove, IL 60515-1426
Internet: www.ivpress.com
E-mail: mail@ivpress.com

InterVarsity Press® is the book-publishing division of InterVarsity Christian Fellowship/USA®, a student movement active on campus at hundreds of universities, colleges and schools of nursing in the United States of America, and a member movement of the International Fellowship of Evangelical Students. For information about local and regional activities, write Public Relations Dept., InterVarsity Christian Fellowship/USA, 6400 Schroeder Rd., P.O. Box 7895, Madison, WI 53707-7895, or visit the IVCF website at <www.intervarsity.org>.

Cover design: Cindy Kiple
Cover image: Erich Lessing/Art Resource, NY

ISBN-10: 0-8308-3322-6
ISBN-13: 978-0-8308-3322-1

Printed in the United States of America ∞

Library of Congress Cataloging-in-Publication Data

Basic Christian leadership/John Stott
    p. cm.
Includes bibliographical references and index.
  ISBN 0-8308-2305-0 (cloth ed., alk. paper)
  ISBN 0-8308-3322-6 (paper ed., alk. paper)
  1. Leadership—Religious aspects—Christianity. I. Title.
  BV4597.53.L43 S76 2002
  253—dc21
                                         2002009225

P	19	18	17	16	15	14	13	12	11	10	9	8	7	6	5	4	3	2	1
Y	21	20	19	18	17	16	15	14	13	12	11	10	09	08	07	06				

CONTENTS

PREFACE

F or forty years and more I have been fascinated and challenged by the early chapters of 1 Corinthians. They have cast their spell over me. I believe they have a special message for church leaders today, whether ordained or lay, whether their ministry is in the world or in the church.

So I have sought to expound these chapters in a variety of contexts: in conferences for clergy and missionaries in North America, Romania and Papua New Guinea; at the biennial conference of FEET (The Fellowship of European Evangelical Theologians); and at meetings for student leaders and theological students in Germany, Poland, Kenya, Argentina and Costa Rica. I have also been privileged to take these chapters for the biblical expositions at the Keswick Convention in the north of England, first in 1962 and then again nearly forty years later in the millennium year, I hope with a greater degree of insight and understanding than previously.

In preparing these expositions for a wider public, I have found the text extraordinarily relevant to Christian leaders in the contemporary world.

Leadership

A leader, according to its simplest definition, is someone who commands a following. To lead is to go ahead, to show the way and to inspire other people to follow.

Leaders are needed in every walk of life. Leadership is not restricted to world statesmen, national top brass, the opinion-formers who dominate the media and the senior executives of multinationals. Leaders can also be influential in their local community: teachers in the school, students in the university, parents in the home and many others.

Leadership is a word shared by Christians and non-Christians alike, but this does not mean that their concept of it is the same. On the contrary, Jesus introduced into the world a new style of servant-leadership. He said:

> *You know that those who are regarded as rulers of the Gentiles lord it over them, and their high officials exercise authority over them.*

Not so with you. Instead, whoever wants to become great among you must be your servant, and whoever wants to be first must be slave of all. (Mk 10:42-44)

The most influential leader in the early church was undoubtedly the apostle Paul. Appointed by Jesus as the apostle to the Gentiles, he never lost his vision of God's single new humanity, Jews and Gentiles together, for which he suffered painful opposition and imprisonment. And in his letters we watch him exercising his leadership skills.

Of course, Paul was an apostle and we are not. Indeed, as I shall argue shortly, there are no apostles in the church today who have an authority comparable to that of the apostle Paul.

Nevertheless, Jesus Christ has evidently intended from the beginning that his church should be shepherded, or have pastoral guidance. So from the first missionary journey onward Paul appointed elders in every church (Acts 14:23), and he later instructed Timothy and Titus to do the same, giving instructions as to what kind of people pastors should be (1 Tim 3:1-13; Tit 1:5-9).

In the first four chapters of 1 Corinthians, which form the basic text of this book, Paul is responding to the complex Corinthian situation and the questions the Corinthians have addressed to him. He does so with admirable clarity, wisdom, humility, love and gentleness: pastoral qualities that are sorely needed by Christian leaders today.

ONE

The Ambiguity
of the Church

1 Corinthians 1:1–17

1 CORINTHIANS 1:1-17

*Paul, called to be an apostle of Christ Jesus by the will of God,
and our brother Sosthenes,*

*To the church of God in Corinth, to those sanctified in Christ
Jesus and called to be holy, together with all those everywhere
who call on the name of our Lord Jesus Christ—their Lord
and ours:*

*Grace and peace to you from God our Father and the Lord
Jesus Christ.*

*I always thank God for you because of his grace given you in
Christ Jesus. For in him you have been enriched in every
way—in all your speaking and in all your knowledge—
because our testimony about Christ was confirmed in you.
Therefore you do not lack any spiritual gift as you eagerly wait
for our Lord Jesus Christ to be revealed. He will keep you
strong to the end, so that you will be blameless on the day of
our Lord Jesus Christ. God, who has called you into fellowship
with his Son Jesus Christ our Lord, is faithful.*

I appeal to you, brothers, in the name of our Lord Jesus Christ, that all of you agree with one another so that there may be no divisions among you and that you may be perfectly united in mind and thought. My brothers, some from Chloe's household have informed me that there are quarrels among you. What I mean is this: One of you says, "I follow Paul"; another, "I follow Apollos"; another, "I follow Cephas"; still another, "I follow Christ."

Is Christ divided? Was Paul crucified for you? Were you baptized into the name of Paul? I am thankful that I did not baptize any of you except Crispus and Gaius, so no one can say that you were baptized into my name. (Yes, I also baptized the household of Stephanas; beyond that, I don't remember if I baptized anyone else.) For Christ did not send me to baptize, but to preach the gospel—not with words of human wisdom, lest the cross of Christ be emptied of its power.

The Ambiguity of the Church

The image of the church presented in the first four chapters of 1 Corinthians is extremely ambiguous. For there is a paradox at the heart of the church. It is the painful tension between what the church *claims* to be and what it *seems* to be; between the divine ideal and the human reality; between romantic talk about "the bride of Christ" and the very unromantic, ugly, unholy and quarrelsome Christian community we know ourselves to be. It is the tension between our final, glorious destiny in heaven and our present, very inglorious performance on earth. This is the ambiguity of the church.

Consider the first two verses of 1 Corinthians, in which Paul describes both himself as the author of the letter and the Corinthian church as its recipient:

> *Paul, called to be an apostle of Christ Jesus by the will of God, and our brother Sosthenes,*
> *To the church of God in Corinth, to those sanctified in Christ Jesus and called to be holy, together with all those everywhere who call on the name of our Lord Jesus Christ—their Lord and ours.*

As for himself, Paul is *called to be an apostle of Christ Jesus by the will of God.* As for the Corinthian church, it is *the church of God in Corinth.* Thus an apostle of Christ is writing to a church of God. Both are privileged and exalted titles.

1. PAUL'S SELF-DESCRIPTION

In nine of the thirteen letters attributed to Paul in the New Testament he identifies himself as Christ's apostle by the will or command of God. How then are we to understand this word *apostle?* It is used in the New Testament in three distinct senses.

Only once is *apostle* used of all the disciples of Jesus indiscriminately, namely in John 13:16, where Jesus says after washing the feet of the Twelve. "I tell you the truth, no servant is greater than his master, nor is a messenger *(apostolos)* greater than the one who sent him." In this general sense we are all apostles, because we are all messengers or ambassadors of Christ sent out into the world with the message of the gospel, sharing together in the apostolic mission of the church (cf. Jn 17:18; 20:21).

Three or four times we read in the New Testament of "apostles of the churches." These were messengers sent out by a particular church on a particular mission, as Epaphroditus was the Philippians' "apostle" ("messenger"; Phil 2:25), and as certain brothers were "representatives *(apostoloi)* of the churches" (2 Cor 8:23). We would probably call them "missionaries" or "mission partners."

The overwhelming use of *apostle* in the New Testament, however, is in relation to the Twelve, whom Jesus himself named apostles (Lk 6:13), and to whom certainly Paul and probably James were later added. They were not "apostles of the churches" but "apostles of Christ." They were a unique group with the following three characteristics.

- They had been personally chosen, called and appointed directly by Jesus Christ, not by any human being or institution.
- They were eyewitnesses of the historical Jesus—either of his public ministry for three years (e.g., Mk 3:14; Jn 15:27) or at least witnesses to his resurrection (e.g., Acts 1:21-22). "Am I not an apostle?" writes Paul later in 1 Corinthians (9:1), and adds immediately the supplementary

question, "Have I not seen Jesus our Lord?" And in the
list of resurrection appearances that Paul gives in chapter 15 he writes: "Last of all he appeared to me also, as to
one abnormally born. For I am the least of the apostles"
(15:8-9).

- They were promised a special inspiration of the Spirit of
  truth, who would both remind them of what Jesus had
  taught them (Jn 14:25-26) and supplement it as he would
  lead them "into all truth" (16:12-15). These great promises
  were fulfilled in the writing of the New Testament.

It is extremely important to maintain these three apostolic
characteristics that gave the apostles their unique authority and
qualified them for their unique ministry as scribes of the New
Testament. Theological liberals are brash enough to say, "That
was Paul's opinion; this is mine." Or, "He was a first-century
witness to Christ; I am a twenty-first-century witness to
Christ." Or, "We wrote the Bible, so we can rewrite it."

But no! We did not write the Bible. The biblical authors did
not write in the name of the church or in their own name. On
the contrary, they wrote to the church in the name of God (the
Old Testament prophets) and in the name of Christ (the New
Testament apostles). This is why we receive the teaching of the
biblical authors "not as the word of men, but as it actually is,
the word of God" (1 Thess 2:13).

So then, as we study these early chapters of 1 Corinthians,
we shall not wander through the text like a gardener through a
herbaceous border, picking the flowers we like and discarding
those we do not like. We shall not behave as if we thought the
New Testament were a collection of the fallible opinions of fallible human beings. We shall rather put ourselves humbly un-

der its authority, and listen attentively to what God has to say to us through his Word.

So much for Paul's self-description. He had been called to be an apostle of Christ. True, he adds a mention of Sosthenes, perhaps the former ruler of the synagogue in Corinth whom Luke mentions (Acts 18:17). And Paul refers to him by name perhaps because he was Paul's scribe, to whom he was dictating this letter, and because Paul was appointing him to carry the letter to Corinth and to read it aloud in the public assembly. Yet Paul designates him only "our brother," not an apostle.

Indeed, we need to have the courage to insist that there are no "apostles of Christ" in the church today. Perhaps some leaders could be described as having apostolic ministries (e.g., bishops, superintendents, pioneer missionaries and church planters). But there is nobody with the authority of the apostles Paul, John, Peter and the others. If there were, we would have to add their teaching to the New Testament.

2. PAUL'S DESCRIPTION OF THE CORINTHIAN CHURCH

Paul says he is writing *to the church of God in Corinth*. The words sound innocent enough at first hearing. But it is extraordinary that such a community should exist in such a city.

What do we know about Corinth? Owing to its political opposition to Rome, Corinth had been destroyed in 146 B.C. But it was rebuilt and refounded as a Roman colony by Julius Caesar about a hundred years later. It owed its distinction mainly to its strategic location on the narrow Corinthian isthmus. Here it commanded the trade routes both north-south by land and east-west by sea. It was therefore both a manufacturing and a trading center. It also played host to the world-famous Isthmian Games, which were held in its huge stadium every two years.

Corinth was also a religious city, honoring "many 'gods' and many 'lords,'" as Paul was to write later (1 Cor 8:5). Among its idolatrous buildings the temple of Aphrodite dominated the Acrocorinth, which rose nearly two thousand feet behind the city, and the temple of Apollo in the town center. At the same time Corinth was an immoral city, so that Aristophanes coined the verb "to corinthianize," meaning "to live a licentious life."

Corinth also had political importance as the capital city of the Roman province of Achaia (southern Greece). Thus Corinth was a busy, thriving, affluent, proud and permissive city. Merchants and sailors, pilgrims and athletes, tourists and prostitutes jostled one another in its narrow streets.

Yet in this heathen city there lived a small group of people whom Paul called *the church of God in Corinth*, the divine community in the human community. It was like a fragrant flower growing in and out of the smelly mud.

Already therefore in verse 2 the ambiguity of the church is indicated—its two habitats (earthly and heavenly, in Corinth and in Christ) and its two sanctities (actual and potential, "sanctified in Christ Jesus and called to be holy"). It also had two callings, for God calls us to be holy, and we call on God to make us holy. Again, God calls us to be the holy people we are, and we call on God to be the unique person he is, according to his name or nature. Indeed, this is the essence of prayer. It is only by calling on God to be himself that we have any hope of becoming more truly ourselves, the holy people of God.

Fundamental to New Testament Christianity is this ambiguity of the church. We are living between times, between the first and second comings of Christ, between what he did when he came and what he will do when he comes again, between kingdom come and kingdom coming, between the "now already" of kingdom inaugurated and the "not yet" of kingdom consummated. It is the key to our understanding of 1 Corinthians and of the Christian life. John Newton expressed it well:

> I am not what I ought to be, I am not what I want to be, I am not what I hope to be in another world. But still I am not what I once used to be, and by the grace of God I am what I am.[1]

Now, having considered the apostle Paul and the Corinthian church separately, it is time to consider them together.

3. PAUL AND CORINTH
Paul had a close, longstanding, personal and pastoral relationship with the Corinthian church. It began in A.D. 50, during his second missionary journey, when he first visited the city and founded its church (2 Cor 10:14). Using the three metaphors that he himself develops in these chapters, we may say that he planted the church, while Apollos and others did the watering (1 Cor 3:6); he laid the foundation, while others erected the superstructure (3:10); he fathered the church, while others were its guardians and tutors (4:14-15). Over the years Paul visited Corinth at least three times and wrote to its church at least four times, although only two of his letters have survived.

Having looked at Paul and Corinth both separately and together, we are now able to return to his letter and to consider what Paul wrote in its first seventeen verses.

- First, Paul greets the church (vv. 1-3).

- Second, Paul gives thanks for the church (vv. 4-9).
- Third, Paul appeals to the church (vv. 10-17).

And in each of these three sections (the greeting, the thanksgiving and the appeal) the apostle singles out one essential characteristic of the church. Each of these characteristics illustrates the church's ambiguity in relation to its holiness (vv. 1-3), its giftedness (vv. 4-9) and its unity (vv. 10-17).

a. Paul greets the church (1:1-3), and in his greeting he emphasizes its holiness. What Paul has called *the church of God in Corinth* he now also identifies as *those sanctified in Christ Jesus* and *those called to be holy.*

The ambiguity is obvious. The church is both already holy and not yet holy. It has been sanctified, and it is called to sanctity. Moreover, this is so of *all those everywhere who call on the name of our Lord Jesus Christ—their Lord and ours.* The addition of these words, writes Anthony Thiselton, "reinforces the thought that the church in Corinth is *not a self-contained autonomous entity: they are not a self-sufficient community; they are not the only pebble on the beach.*"[2] On the contrary, they are part of God's worldwide community.

On the one hand, the Corinthian community is "the church of God." Like Israel before it, it is God's holy people. Its members have been set apart to belong to God. On the other hand, as the coming chapters will make clear, much unholiness remains in the holy people: quarrelling, pride, complacency, immorality, taking one another to court, disorders in public worship and boastfulness in relation to their spiritual gifts. For this mixed-up community Paul wishes and prays *Grace and peace . . . from God our Father and the Lord Jesus Christ* (v. 3).

b. Paul gives thanks for the church (1:4-9), and in his thanksgiving he emphasizes its giftedness. In spite of the Corinthian church's many failures, Paul begins with a positive evaluation: *I always thank God for you.* For what does he give thanks? First *because of his grace given you in Christ Jesus* (v. 4), which is surely a reference to their salvation by God's sheer grace. But he also thanks God that in Christ *you have been enriched in every way—in all your speaking and in all your knowledge* (v. 5; that is, their understanding and ability to communicate it). Next Paul reminds them that his apostolic *testimony about Christ* had been *confirmed* in them (v. 6), since what he had taught about Christ had proved to be true. And in consequence, they *do not lack any spiritual gift* (v. 7).

It is a remarkable expression of thanksgiving to God that the Corinthians had received his saving grace in Christ, that they had been enriched in every way and that they therefore lacked no spiritual gift. It sounds as if the Corinthian church is perfect—in every way enriched, in no way deficient. It appears to be complete. (Not of course that each individual Christian has all spiritual gifts—1 Corinthians 12 will make that plain—but each local church, as the body of Christ, may expect to be given collectively all the gifts it needs.)

And yet this is not the end of the story. Even though the Corinthian church has been wonderfully graced and enriched in every way in Christ so that it lacks nothing, it is still not blameless. That is why they still *eagerly wait for our Lord Jesus Christ to be revealed* (v. 7). Not only will he keep them *strong to the end,* but in consequence they *will be blameless* on that day (v. 8). Enriched now, we shall be blameless then. We know this not because of our faith but because of God's faithfulness. *God, who has called you into fellowship with his Son Jesus Christ our Lord, is faithful* (v. 9). It is a pity that in this rendering the adjective *faithful* comes last in the sentence, since in the Greek it comes first: "Faithful is God who . . ." Having called us into fellowship with Christ, into our common participation in Christ, he will one day perfect our participation in him. "God called us" is a past reality. "Fellowship with Christ" is the present experience. "God is faithful" is the ground of our confidence for the future.

c. Paul appeals to the church (1:10-17), and in his appeal he emphasizes its unity. Before we are ready to consider the divisions in the Corinthian church, we need to glance back to the beginning of verse 2, where Paul addresses *the church of God.* Doubtless God says to himself, *I have only one church.* As Paul later teaches in his letter to the Ephesians, there is only one family because there is only one Father; there is only one body because there is only one Spirit who indwells it; and there is only one faith, hope and baptism because there is only one Lord who is the object of them all (Eph 4:4-6). Similarly, in 1 Corinthians Paul will later write, "you are God's field" (3:9), "God's temple" (3:16) , "the body of Christ" (12:27). These are collective nouns that all declare the unity of the church. There may have been several house churches in Corinth, but if so, Paul still thinks of them as "the church of God," one and undivided.

Yet the Corinthians had succeeded in dividing the indivisible! They were tearing the church apart by their factions. Paul has given thanks for them; now he appeals to them. He has been affirming them; now he reproves them. He turns from their enrichment in Christ to their fragmentation from one another.

What can we learn from the apostle's appeal? First, we notice that twice he addresses them as *brothers* (vv. 10, 11). He reminds them of the family of God to which they belonged but which they were contradicting by their behavior. Next he makes the basis of his appeal the name of Christ: *I appeal to you, brothers, in the name of our Lord Jesus Christ* (v. 10). It is the name on which all Christians call (v. 2) and the name into which all Christians are baptized (vv. 13, 15). They named human names, claiming their patronage (v. 12); but, as Chrysostom wrote, "Paul keeps nailing them to the name of Christ."[3]

Here is his appeal: *that all of you agree with one another so that there may be no divisions among you and that you may be perfectly united in mind and thought* (v. 10). Next he goes into more detail. Some members of *Chloe's household* (evidently known to him and them, though not to us) had informed him *that there are quarrels among you* (v. 11). That is, *one of you says, "I follow Paul"; another, "I follow Apollos"; another, "I follow Cephas [Peter]"; still another, "I follow Christ"* (v. 12).

There is much discussion about the identity of these rival groups. Some try to find different theologies in contradiction with one another. The most famous of these was the theory of F. C. Baur, the nineteenth-century professor of New Testament at Tübingen. He argued that in the early church there was a fundamental opposition between Gentile Christianity (headed by Paul) and Jewish Christianity (headed by Peter). He found support for his thesis in these verses of 1 Corinthians, and went on to interpret the whole New Testament in the light of an ongoing tension between Paul and Peter.

But there is no evidence in our text that these groups were divided by doctrine. No, the issue in Corinth concerned personalities, not principles. The groups were separated from each other by a celebrity cult, by pride, jealousy and boastfulness, which deeply distressed Paul. He was their brother (vv. 10, 11), not their master. If anybody "belonged" to anybody, he belonged to them, not they to him (cf. 3:22-23).

What, then, about the fourth slogan, "I follow Christ" or "I belong to Christ"? How could one faction claim to have a monopoly in Christ? All Christians belong to Christ, not to a clique. Some therefore suggest that, although the first three were the slogans of different Corinthian factions, the fourth is not another but Paul's own indignant retort: "As for me, I belong to Christ" (cf. 2 Cor 10:7).

Consider now the seriousness of the situation in the Corinthian church. Although the divisions were not doctrinal in origin, they had profound doctrinal implications, especially in relation to Christ and the gospel. In order to show this, in 1:13 Paul asks three leading questions, all of which demand as an answer an emphatic, uncompromising "No!"

> Question 1: Is Christ divided? That is, "Is there more than one Christ?" (J. B. Phillips). Or "Has Christ been shared out?"[4] with fragments of him distributed between different groups? No! The very idea is preposterous. There is only one Christ.

> Question 2: Was Paul crucified for you? Were they trusting for their salvation in Paul and him crucified? No! The idea is ludicrous, almost blasphemous. Jesus Christ alone is our crucified Savior, in whom we have put our trust.

> Question 3: Were you baptized into the name of Paul? No, of course not! Baptism is into allegiance to Christ. As the apostle emphasizes in Romans 6, we have been baptized into union with Christ crucified and risen.

Thus the effect of the Corinthian divisions was to undermine the essentials of the gospel. It was to deny that there is only one Christ, who was crucified for us and into whose name we have been baptized. Clearly, the person of Christ, the cross of Christ and the name of Christ are all at stake when the church is divided. The Corinthians were effectively insulting Christ by dislodging him from his supremacy and replacing him with human leaders.

In verses 14-17 Paul lingers on the topic of baptism because the Corinthians were putting their emphasis in the wrong place. They were exalting the human baptizer at the expense of the divine Christ, into whom they had been baptized. Consequently, Paul expresses thankfulness for what he saw as the providence of God in "a simple, uncalculated, historical reality."[5] This was that he had not baptized any of them, except (he adds) Crispus the synagogue ruler (Acts 18:8) and Gaius, who became the church's host (Rom 16:23). In consequence, *no one can say that you were baptized into my name* (1 Cor 1:15). *Yes,* he adds as an afterthought, even a parenthesis, *I also baptized the household of Stephanas* (cf. 16:15, 17); *beyond that, I don't remember if I baptized anyone else* (1:16).

His inability to remember exactly whom he had baptized indicates how comparatively unimportant the question was. For what matters in our baptism is not the person by whom but the person into whom we were baptized. Besides, Paul adds, *Christ did not send me* (or "apostle" me) *to baptize, but to preach the gospel* (v. 17). He is not being derogatory to baptism. He knew that baptism had been instituted by Jesus as an integral part of the Great Commission, and he himself had a high view of the importance and significance of baptism, as is plain in Romans 6.

But his speciality as an apostle of Christ was evangelism, not baptism; pioneer preaching, not local-church pastoring; the gospel, not the sacraments that dramatize it visibly.

Moreover, the evangelism Paul was commissioned to do was *not with words of human wisdom* (literally 'not in wisdom of word'), *lest the cross of Christ be emptied of its power* (1 Cor 1:17). This is a very important statement, not least because it antici-pates the developed argument of 1:18—2:5, which we shall consider in the next chapter. The phrase "not in wisdom of word" expresses a double renunciation. On the one hand, Paul renounced the world's wisdom in favor of the cross of Christ. On the other hand, he renounced "the skills of rhetoric" (Re-vised English Bible) for the power of God. The Jerusalem Bible brings the two together in a footnote referring to "philosophical speculation and tricks of rhetoric." This double renunciation of human philosophy and human rhetoric Paul elaborates later. As C. H. Hodge put it, "He was neither a philosopher, nor a rhetorician after the Grecian school."[6]

CONCLUSION

The opening section of 1 Corinthians obliges us to reflect on the ambiguity of the church and to come to terms with it.

On the one hand, biblical Christians are not perfectionists who dream of developing a perfect church on earth. As Billy Graham has often wisely said, "By all means look for the perfect church, and when you find it, join it. But remember, when you join it, it ceases to be perfect!" On the other hand, biblical Christians are not defeatists who tolerate all manner of sin and error in the church.

To perfectionists we say, "You are right to seek the purity of the church. The doctrinal and ethical purity of the church is a proper goal of Christian endeavor. But you are wrong to imagine that you will attain it. Not till Christ comes will he present his bride to himself as 'a radiant church, without stain or wrinkle or any other blemish, but holy and blameless' (Eph 5:27)."

To defeatists we say, "You are right to acknowledge the reality of sin and error in the church, and not to close your eyes to it. But you are wrong to tolerate it. There is a place for discipline in the church, and even for excommunication. To deny the divine-human person of Jesus Christ is antichrist (1 John 2:22). To deny the gospel of grace is to deserve God's anathema (Gal 1:6-9). We cannot condone these things."

So this is the ambiguity of the church.

- The church is sanctified yet still sinful and called to be holy.
- The church is enriched yet still defective, eagerly waiting for the return of Christ.
- The church is united (the one and only church of God) yet still unnecessarily divided and called to renounce personality cults.

In these ways we are living in the painful tension between the already and the not yet. Only when Christ comes will the ideal become reality, and all ambiguity cease.

TWO

Power Through

Weakness

1 Corinthians 1:18—2:5

1 CORINTHIANS 1:18 — 2:5

For the message of the cross is foolishness to those who are

perishing, but to us who are being saved it is the power of God.

For it is written:

"I will destroy the wisdom of the wise;

the intelligence of the intelligent I will frustrate."

Where is the wise man? Where is the scholar? Where is the

philosopher of this age? Has not God made foolish the wisdom

of the world? For since in the wisdom of God the world through

its wisdom did not know him, God was pleased through the

foolishness of what was preached to save those who believe.

Jews demand miraculous signs and Greeks look for wisdom,

but we preach Christ crucified: a stumbling block to Jews and

foolishness to Gentiles, but to those whom God has called, both

Jews and Greeks, Christ the power of God and the wisdom of

God. For the foolishness of God is wiser than man's wisdom,

and the weakness of God is stronger than man's strength.

Brothers, think of what you were when you were called. Not many of you were wise by human standards; not many were influential; not many were of noble birth. But God chose the foolish things of the world to shame the wise; God chose the weak things of the world to shame the strong. He chose the lowly things of this world and the despised things—and the things that are not—to nullify the things that are, so that no one may boast before him. It is because of him that you are in Christ Jesus, who has become for us wisdom from God—that is, our righteousness, holiness and redemption. Therefore, as it is written: "Let him who boasts boast in the Lord."

When I came to you, brothers, I did not come with eloquence or superior wisdom as I proclaimed to you the testimony about God. For I resolved to know nothing while I was with you except Jesus Christ and him crucified. I came to you in weakness and fear, and with much trembling. My message and my preaching were not with wise and persuasive words, but with a demonstration of the Spirit's power, so that your faith might not rest on men's wisdom, but on God's power.

Power Through Weakness

At first sight 1 Corinthians 1:17—2:5 focuses on power.

- Paul fears "lest the cross of Christ be emptied of its *power*" (1:17).
- "For the message of the cross," he continues, "is . . . to us who are being saved . . . the *power* of God" (1:18).
- "To those whom God has called . . . Christ [is] the *power* of God" (1:24).
- "My message and my preaching were . . . with a demonstration of the Spirit's *power*" (2:4).
- This was "so that your faith might . . . rest . . . on God's *power*" (2:5).

Further, for the sake of completeness, we must add two verses from 2 Corinthians.

- "We have this treasure in jars of clay to show that this all-surpassing *power* is from God" (2 Cor 4:7).
- The Lord said to Paul, "My *power* is made perfect in weakness." In consequence, the apostle said he would boast in his weaknesses "so that Christ's *power* may rest on me" (2 Cor 12:9).

Here are eight references to power: the power of God, the power of Christ, the power of the cross and the power of the Spirit.

This concentration on power makes an immediate appeal to us today, for we live in a society that worships power. Not that this is new. The lust for power has always been a characteristic of the human story, at least since Adam and Eve were offered power in exchange for disobedience.

Still today the three major human ambitions (the pursuit of money, fame and influence) are all concealed drives for power. Indeed, we see this thirst for power everywhere—in politics and public life, in civil conflict and the resort to arms, in big business and industry, in the professions in which professional expertise threatens those without it, and in primitive societies in which the shaman or witchdoctor trades secret power for money.

Unfortunately, we see the same power-hunger in the church: in top-level ecclesiastical power struggles, in denominational disputes, in some local churches driven by market forces and others in which the clergy hold all the reins of power and refuse to share it with the lay people (and especially the young people), in parachurch organizations that dream of expanding into world empires and even in the pulpit, which is an exceedingly dangerous place for any child of Adam to occupy.

Power! It is more intoxicating than alcohol, more addictive than drugs. It was Lord Acton, the nineteenth-century British politician, friend and adviser of Prime Minister William Gladstone, who composed the epigram "Power tends to corrupt; absolute power corrupts absolutely." Acton was very disturbed in his day to see democracy being undermined by power struggles. He was also a Roman Catholic who, in 1870, strongly opposed the decision of the First Vatican Council to attribute infallibility to the pope. He saw it as power corrupting the church.

Turning from the Roman Catholic to the evangelical scene, I confess to being frightened by the contemporary evangelical hunger for power, even the quest for the power of the Holy Spirit. Why do we want to receive power? Is it honestly power for witness (as in Acts 1:8) or holiness or humble service? Or is it in reality a mask for personal ambition, a craving to boost our own ego, to minister to our self-importance, to impress, to dominate or to manipulate?

Even some evangelism is a disguised form of imperialism, since it builds human empires instead of the kingdom of God. Only one imperialism is Christian, and that is a concern for His Imperial Majesty the Lord Jesus Christ, a longing for the glory of his kingdom, for the honor of his name.

So the Bible contains clear warnings about the use and abuse of power. In the Old Testament we read about Uzziah (alias Azariah), king of Judah, that "he was greatly helped until he became powerful. But after Uzziah became powerful, his pride led to his downfall" (2 Chron 26:15-16). In the New Testament the Lord Jesus himself warns the apostles against exercising the "authority" and "lordship" that characterize leadership in the secular community. "Not so with you," he declared, for Christian leadership is marked rather by humility and service (Mk 10:42-44). And the apostle Peter clearly echoed this teaching when he urged church elders to shepherd God's people, "not greedy for money, but eager to serve; not lording it over those entrusted to you, but being examples to the flock" (1 Pet 5:2-3).

At no point does the Christian mind come into more violent collision with the secular mind than in its insistence on humility, with all the weakness it entails. The wisdom of the world values power, not humility. We have drunk in more of the power philosophy of Friedrich Nietzsche than we realize. Nietzsche dreamed of the rise of a daring ruler-race—tough, masculine and oppressive. Nietzsche worshiped power; he despised Jesus for his weakness. The ideal of Nietzsche was the *Übermensch*, the superman; but the ideal of Jesus was the little child. There is no possibility of compromise between these two images; we are obliged to choose.

After this long introduction, we are ready to return to the central theme of Paul's Corinthian correspondence, which is not power (as you might think at first sight) but power through weakness, divine power through human weakness. Paul brings together in 1 Corinthians 1—2 three striking illustrations of the same principle.

- First, we see power through weakness *in the gospel itself*, for the weakness of the cross is the power of God (1:17-25, especially vv. 18, 24).
- Second, we see power through weakness *in the Corinthian converts*, for God had chosen weak people to shame the strong (1:26-31, especially v. 27).
- Third, we see power through weakness *in Paul the evangelist*, for "I came to you," he said, "in weakness and fear" but "with a demonstration of the Spirit's power" (2:1-5, especially vv. 3-4).

Thus the gospel, the converts and the preacher (or the evangel, the evangelized and the evangelist) all exhibited the same principle. God's power operates best in human weakness. Weakness is the arena in which God can most effectively manifest his power. Consider now how Paul develops his threefold theme.

1. POWER THROUGH WEAKNESS IN THE GOSPEL ITSELF (1:18-25)

Every communicator has to answer two basic questions. First, what have I got to say? Second, how shall I say it? The first concerns the message we have to communicate, the second the method of our communication.

In the first-century world of Greco-Roman culture these two questions received a ready answer. The "what" of communication was philosophy, and the "how" was rhetoric, an elaborate ornamentation of language and style. Moreover the Corinthians (even after their conversion) were still enamored of popular rhetoric. They thought of the gospel as *sōphia* (wisdom), and they considered that it should be presented with appropriate ornamentation. Paul strongly disagreed. He renounced them both. He refused to preach the gospel "in wisdom of word" (as in v. 17). In place of human philosophy and human rhetoric he put the cross, for the cross is both the wisdom of God and the power of God. Paul now enlarges on his position twice over, first in verses 18-21 and second in verses 22-25. In both paragraphs he begins with the cross (vv. 18, 23), and in both he continues with the different responses people make to the message of the cross.

Verses 18-21. The message of the cross receives diametrically opposed reactions. It is *foolishness to those who are perishing, but to us who are being saved it is the power of God* (v. 18). And Paul endorses this from Scripture. He quotes from Isaiah 29:14 to the effect that God destroys and frustrates human wisdom, and even makes it foolish (1 Cor 1:19-20).

What comes next is a beautifully chiseled sentence. Verse 21 rests on the fundamental fact that human beings cannot reach God by themselves. On the one hand, God is infinite, whereas we are finite. On the other hand, God is holy, whereas we are sinners. In consequence, we are doubly cut off from God. So God has taken the initiative to do what we cannot do, namely, to bridge the gulf between us.

In order to explain this, verse 21 contains three contrasts that emerge when we ask three questions.

Question 1: Who took the initiative to reach us? Answer: God did. For since in the wisdom of God the world through its wisdom did not (and could not) know him, God was pleased to take saving action on our behalf.

Question 2: What was the result of God's initiative? Answer: Salvation. God was pleased . . . to save those who believe.

Question 3: How was the initiative taken? Answer: Through the gospel. For since the world failed to reach God through its own wisdom, God was pleased to save us through the foolishness of what was preached (the **kērygma** or message).

Here then is the summary of verse 21. Wherever the world failed through its own wisdom to know God, God was pleased to save believers through the folly of the gospel. The contrast stands out starkly between the world and God, between not knowing God and being saved, and between the world's wisdom and the foolishness of the gospel.

Verses 22-25. In the next paragraph Paul elaborates the same thesis: wisdom through the folly of the cross and power through the weakness of the cross. In order to do so, however, he divides the human race into three sections—Jews, Greeks and Christians—and pinpoints the essential differences between them.

First, *Jews demand miraculous signs* (v. 22). They were expecting a political Messiah who would drive the Roman legions into the Mediterranean Sea and reestablish the lost national sovereignty of Israel. So from every revolutionary pretender they demanded appropriate evidence, especially signs of power, to give plausibility to his messianic claims. That is why they kept asking Jesus, "What signs do you do that we may believe?" (e.g., Mt 12:38; 16:1; Mk 8:11; Lk 11:16; Jn 2:18; 4:48; 6:30).

Second, *Greeks look for wisdom* (1 Cor 1:22). Greece had had a long tradition of brilliant philosophy. The Greeks believed in the autonomy of the human mind. So they listened eagerly to every new idea, every speculation, so long as it seemed to them "reasonable."

So Jews demanded power and Greeks sought wisdom. As Gordon Fee has put it, "The demand for power and the insistence on wisdom . . . are still the basic idolatries of our fallen world."[1]

Over against "the wonder-seeking Jew" and "the wisdom-seeking Greek"[2] there is a third category, namely, Christian believers. *We preach Christ crucified* (v. 23). Notice the contrast implied in the three verbs. Jews "make demands," and Greeks are "seeking." What then is the characteristic of Christian preachers? It is neither "demanding" nor "searching" but "proclaiming" the gospel of Christ crucified.

But "a crucified Messiah was an *oxymoron*, a contradiction in terms,"[3] a uniting of opposites. For "Messiah meant power, splendor, triumph; crucifixion meant weakness, humiliation, defeat."[4]No wonder the message of "Christ crucified" provoked different reactions.

First, Christ crucified was *a stumbling block to Jews* (v. 23). They were expecting a powerful military Messiah riding on a war horse at the head of an army. What were they offered instead? A pathetic, crucified weakling! It was an insult to their national pride. How could God's Messiah end his life under the condemnation of his own people and even under the curse of God? It was impossible. The cross was an absolute stumbling block to those who worshiped power.

Second, Christ crucified was *foolishness to Gentiles* (v. 23). Crucifixion in the Roman world was not only a painful execution; it was a public humiliation. It was reserved for the dregs of society, slaves and criminals. No free man or citizen was ever crucified. It was inconceivable therefore that God's Son should end his life on a gibbet. In his eloquent speeches Cicero several times spoke of the horror of crucifixion. For example, "The very name of the cross is absent not only from the body of Roman citizens, but also from their mind, eyes and ears."[5] In other words, citizens would never even look at, listen to or think about a crucifixion.

Third, Christ crucified was *to those whom God has called, both Jews and Greeks, . . . the power of God and the wisdom of God* (v. 24). In spite of what the cross may seem to be, it was not weakness but God's power, not foolishness but God's wisdom. *For the foolishness of God is wiser than man's wisdom, and the weakness of God is stronger than man's strength* (v. 25).

It may be good now to pause and reflect on the contemporary application of Paul's thesis. This whole text is embarrassingly relevant today. To be sure, there are no first-century Jews or Greeks in the world, but there are many modern equivalents.

First, *the cross is still a stumbling block to all who*, like Nietzsche, *worship power* and are confident in their own power to save themselves, or at least to contribute substantially to their salvation. Like the Jews of Paul's day, they seek to establish their own righteousness (Rom 10:3). They imagine that they can accumulate merit and so put God in their debt. But the cross tells them it is impossible. Christ died to save us precisely because we cannot save ourselves, and if we could, then "Christ died for nothing" (Gal 2:21).

Second, *the cross is still folly to the intellectually proud.* It makes no sense to them. One example may suffice: the late A. J. Ayer (later Sir Alfred Ayer), Oxford University philosopher and author of *Language, Truth and Logic,* was scathing in his denunciation of Christianity. He was especially scornful of the cross. In an article in *The Guardian* he wrote that of all the historic religions there is a strong case for regarding Christianity as the worst. Why? Because it rested on "the allied doctrines of original sin and vicarious atonement, which are intellectually contemptible and morally outrageous."[6]

Third, *the cross is still to God's people the power of God and the wisdom of God.* It is the power of God because through it God saves those who cannot save themselves. It is the wisdom of God because through it God has solved not only *our* problem (sin and guilt) but *his own.* It is not wrong to speak of a divine problem or dilemma solved at the cross. It arises from God's character of holy love. How could he express his holiness in punishing evil without compromising his love? How could he express his love in forgiving sinners without compromising his justice? How could he be at one and the same time "a righteous God and a Savior" (Is 45:21)? His answer to these questions was and still is the cross. For on the cross he took our place, bore our sin, died our death and so paid our debt.

Thus on the cross God demonstrated both his justice (Rom 3:25) and his love (5:8). And in this double demonstration the wisdom of God is displayed: his wisdom in the foolishness of the cross, his power in its weakness.

2. POWER THROUGH WEAKNESS IN THE CORINTHIAN CONVERTS (1:26-31)

Paul has been inviting the Corinthian Christians to reflect on the gospel and its weakness; now he invites them to reflect on themselves and their own weakness. *Brothers*, he dictates, or "my dear Christian family," as Anthony Thiselton renders the word,[7] *think of what you were when you were called.* He proceeds to remind them. *Not many of you were wise by human standards; not many were influential; not many were of noble birth* (v. 26). That is to say, wisdom and power were not conspicuous among the Corinthian Christians. Indeed, the opposite was the case. *God chose the weak things of the world to shame the strong. He chose the lowly things of this world and the despised things—and the things that are not—to nullify the things that are* (vv. 27-28). The same theme is evident in them as in the cross, namely, wisdom through folly and power through weakness.

What was the purpose of this divine action? Why did God choose foolish, weak and lowly people? It was *so that no one may boast before him* (v. 29). The credit for their salvation belonged to God alone. *It is because of him* (God) *that you are in Christ Jesus* (v. 30). God the Father had united them to Christ, and so (Paul now associates himself with them) Christ *has become for us* on the one hand *wisdom from God* and on the other hand *our righteousness, holiness and redemption* (v. 30). These three great blessings we enjoy in Christ are surely the three tenses of salvation: past (our justification), present (our sanctification) and future (our glorification, including the redemption of our bodies; cf. Rom 8:23; Eph 1:14; 4:30). They are due to God's sheer grace, to his wisdom and power displayed in and through Christ crucified.

Therefore, Paul concludes his argument, *as it is written: "Let him who boasts boast in the Lord"* (v. 31), for all other boasting is excluded. As Jeremiah put it:

> *Let not the wise man boast of his wisdom*
> *or the strong man boast of his strength*
> *or the rich man boast of his riches,*
> *but let him who boasts boast about this:*
> *that he understands and knows me,*
> *that I am the LORD. (Jer 9:23)*

It is evident from these verses that most of the Corinthian converts were drawn from the lower ranks of society. Mostly they did not belong to the intelligentsia, or to the city's influential leaders, or to its aristocracy. No, on the whole they would be regarded as uneducated, insignificant, poor and socially despised, being probably slaves (cf. 1 Cor 7:21). The fact that the gospel reached, saved and changed them was another dramatic illustration of the principle of power through weakness—God's power exhibited in human weakness.

Is the apostle saying that God never calls and saves people who are clever, wealthy, influential or socially prominent? Clearly not. Saul of Tarsus, with his brilliant intellect, was himself an exception to his own rule. Even in Corinth, Luke tells us, Crispus (the ruler of the synagogue) was converted (Acts 18:8). And in Romans 16:23-24 (a letter written from Corinth) Paul sends greetings from both Gaius (wealthy enough to give hospitality to the whole church) and Erastus (described as "the city's director of public works"). Moreover, both 1 and 2 Corinthians imply that some Corinthian Christians were well-to-do (cf. 1 Cor 11:22; 16:2, 15, 19; 2 Cor 8—9).

The key to interpreting these verses is that Paul does not write "not *any* of you" but "not *many* of you." Origen, the mid-third-century church father, noticed this. When Celsus, an early critic, sneered that Christianity was for the uneducated, the stupid and the ignorant, Origen pointed out Paul's phrase "not many." Then Selina, Countess of Huntingdon, the eighteenth-century evangelical aristocrat and friend of John Wesley and George Whitefield who sought to introduce the British upper classes to the gospel, said, "I thank God for the letter 'm' in 'many.'"[8]

What then are we to conclude from this text? Is it wrong to take the gospel to such elitist groups as students and professional people? No, it is not wrong. Paul's emphasis is that God's power operates only in the salvation of the weak. Therefore, if the strong hope to be saved, they must acknowledge their weakness. Otherwise the grace of God cannot reach them. As Jesus put it, the kingdom of God belongs only to children. If therefore adults want to enter it, they have to become like children themselves (Mk 10:13-16).

Luther understood this well:

> *Only the prisoner shall be free;*
> *Only the poor shall be rich;*
> *Only the weak shall be strong;*
> *Only the humble exalted;*
> *Only the empty filled;*
> *Only nothing shall be something.*[9]

3. POWER THROUGH WEAKNESS IN THE EVANGELIST (2:1-5)

Not only were Paul's Corinthian converts weak and feeble, but he, the apostle, though in a somewhat different sense, was weak and feeble too. As Hudson Taylor affirmed in the nineteenth century, "all God's giants have been weak people."[10] This was in contrast to the false teachers, whom Paul dubbed "super-apostles" (2 Cor 11:5). They were proud and self-confident, and boasted of their wisdom, authority and power.

It is necessary to understand the cultural background to the situation in Corinth, especially in regard to rhetoric. "Rhetoric was a systematic, academic discipline taught and practised throughout the Graeco-Roman world."[11] In fact, in the first century A.D. "rhetoric became the primary discipline in Roman higher education."[12] In public debates, in the law courts and at funerals "the rhetoric of display and ornamentation" was tremendously popular as "a form of public entertainment."[13] Gradually it "became an end in itself, mere ornamentation, with a desire to please the crowd . . . but without serious content or intent."[14] A "sophist" was an orator who "emphasized style over substance,"[15] form over content. The goal was applause, the motive vanity and the casualty truth.[16] "It is difficult for us at the end of the twentieth century," wrote Donald Carson, "to appreciate how influential this allegiance to rhetoric was."[17]

So this was the situation in Corinth. The Corinthians had assimilated the rhetorical culture of the day and were evaluating Paul's speech according to the commonly accepted criteria. But Paul made a double negative resolve, which he repeated. He determined to preach in Corinth *not with words of human wisdom* (1:17) and *not with eloquence or superior wisdom* (2:1), which Anthony Thiselton renders "not with high-sounding rhetoric or a display of cleverness."[18]

In both texts Paul uses the same vocabulary: *sōphia* (wisdom, i.e., human philosophy) and *logos* (utterance, i.e., human rhetoric). The Corinthians loved both, but Paul rejected both. In place of human philosophy he *resolved to know nothing while he was with them except Jesus Christ and him crucified* (2:2). In place of human rhetoric he came to them *in weakness and fear, and with much trembling* (v. 3), or "nervous and rather shaky" (J. B. Phillips). In consequence he relied on *a demonstration of the Spirit's power* (v. 4).

I fear that these words would not be an accurate description of many contemporary evangelists. Weakness is not their most obvious characteristic. No, seminary homiletics classes aim to inculcate self-confidence in nervous students. If Paul had enrolled in one of our seminaries today, he would have been regarded as very unpromising material. Since he was supposed to be a mature Christian, we might even have rebuked him, saying "Paul, you've no business to feel nervous. Don't you know what it means to be filled with the Spirit? You ought to be strong, confident, bold!"

But Paul was of a different opinion. He was not afraid to admit that he was afraid. True, he had a massive intellect and a powerful personality. But he was physically frail (whatever his "thorn in the flesh" may have been, 2 Cor 12:7) and emotionally vulnerable (prone to the ups and downs of fluctuating feelings). According to a second-century tradition he was unattractive, small, even ugly, with bald head, beetle brows, bandy legs and a hooked nose.[19] Moreover, his critics said that his bodily presence was weak and his speech contemptible (10:10). So he was nothing much to look at or to listen to. These disabilities would have disqualified him from succeeding as a sophist or rhetorician, or as a popular evangelist today.

Consequently Paul looked elsewhere for his enabling. In his human weakness he relied on the power of God, on *a demonstration of the Spirit's power* (1 Cor 2:4). "It is possible but not probable," writes Gordon Fee, "given the context of 'weakness,' that it [the demonstration of power] reflects the 'signs and wonders' of 2 Corinthians 12:12. More likely it refers to their actual conversion."[20] For every conversion involves a power encounter between Christ and Satan, in which the superior power of Christ is seen. The Holy Spirit takes the evangelist's words, spoken in human weakness, and carries them home with power to the mind, heart, conscience and will of the hearers, in such a way that they see and believe. This is the powerful *apodeixis* (demonstration or proof) of the Spirit.

We must not misunderstand this reference to human weakness. It is not an invitation to suppress our God-given personality, to pretend we feel weak when we do not or to cultivate a fake frailty. Nor is it an exhortation to renounce arguments, since Luke tells us that Paul continued to argue and persuade when he reached Corinth (Acts 18:4-5), and Paul later summed up his evangelistic ministry with the words "we . . . persuade men" (2 Cor 5:11). No, to agree that arguments are insufficient is not to say that they are unnecessary. The Holy Spirit brings people to Christ not in spite of the evidence but because of it, when he opens their eyes to attend to it. Here then is an honest, humble acknowledgment that human beings cannot save souls. Only the power of God can give sight to the blind and life to the dead. But he does it through the gospel of Christ crucified, proclaimed in the power of the Holy Spirit. In other words, the power in every power encounter is in the cross of Christ (for content) and in the Holy Spirit (for communication), irrespective of the weakness of the evangelist.

Perhaps an illustration or two would be in order. C. H. Spurgeon is a notable historical example of the "power through weakness" principle. In his early years as a preacher he sometimes stuttered. All his life he struggled with depression. Later he had regular attacks of gout and occasionally was in such pain while preaching that he had to put one knee on a chair and cling to the pulpit rail. Usually, he said, he felt "terribly sick" before preaching, as if he were crossing the English Channel. And in addition to these physical symptoms, he suffered slanderous attacks from the press. He was only nineteen when he came to London. The *Saturday Review* called him "a coarse, stupid, irrational bigot" and later "an ignorant, conceited fanatic." Many cartoons and caricatures made fun of him. But he persevered, and astonishing power attended his ministry.[21]

Although I am of course no Spurgeon, perhaps I may share an anecdote from my own experience. In 1958 I was privileged to lead an eight-day mission in the University of Sydney, Australia. On the last night the meeting was due to be held in the imposing great hall of the university. But I had caught what the Australians call a "wog" (bug) which had deprived me of speech. Shortly before the meeting some student leaders gathered around me, and one of them read the words of Jesus to Paul: "My grace is sufficient for you, for my power is made perfect in weakness." "Therefore," Paul continues, "I will boast all the more gladly about my weaknesses, so that Christ's power may rest on me. . . . For when I am weak, then I am strong" (2 Cor 12:9-10). Then the students prayed that these words might be fulfilled in me that night.

The hall was packed. But I could only croak my address into

the microphone in a monotone, unable to assert my personality or modulate my voice in any way. When the time came for the invitation, however, there was an immediate and eager response. I have been back in Australia ten times since then, and every time somebody has accosted me somewhere, asking, "Do you remember that meeting in the great hall of Sydney University when you had lost your voice? I came to Christ that night."

CONCLUSION

The central theme of Paul's Corinthian correspondence, and especially of 1 Corinthians 1:17—2:5, is "power through weakness." We have a weak message (Christ crucified), proclaimed by weak preachers (full of fear and trembling), received by weak hearers (the socially despised). For God chose a weak instrument (Paul), to bring a weak message (the cross) to weak people (the Corinthian working class). But through this triple weakness the power of God was—and still is—displayed.

We see this principle supremely in Jesus Christ and his cross. For when in the Judean desert the devil offered him power, he declined the offer. Instead, he gave himself voluntarily to the ultimate weakness and humiliation of the cross. Therefore God has exalted him to the supreme place of power and authority in the universe.

Further, according to Revelation 4—7, at the very center of God's throne (symbol of power) stands a slain Lamb (symbol of weakness). In other words, power through weakness, dramatized in the Lamb on the throne or God on the cross, lies at the very heart of ultimate reality, even of the very being of God himself.

So may this mind be in us which was—and still is—in Christ

Jesus. The Christian leaders needed in the world and the church today are those who have seen the Lamb on the throne and are determined to follow him wherever he goes (Rev 14:4); they know that God's power will be exhibited not in displays of power but in their weakness.

THREE

Holy Spirit and

Holy Scripture

1 Corinthians 2:6-16

1 CORINTHIANS 2:6-16

We do, however, speak a message of wisdom among the mature, but not the wisdom of this age or of the rulers of this age, who are coming to nothing. No, we speak of God's secret wisdom, a wisdom that has been hidden and that God destined for our glory before time began. None of the rulers of this age understood it, for if they had, they would not have crucified the Lord of glory. However, as it is written:

"No eye has seen,

no ear has heard,

no mind has conceived

what God has prepared for those who love him"—

but God has revealed it to us by his Spirit.

The Spirit searches all things, even the deep things of God. For who among men knows the thoughts of a man except the man's spirit within him? In the same way no one knows the thoughts of God except the Spirit of God. We have not received the spirit of the world but the Spirit who is from God, that we may understand what God has freely given us. This is what we speak, not in words taught us by human wisdom but in words taught by the Spirit, expressing spiritual truths in spiritual words. The man without the Spirit does not accept the things that come from the Spirit of God, for they are foolishness to him, and he cannot understand them, because they are spiritually discerned. The spiritual man makes judgments about all things, but he himself is not subject to any man's judgment:

"For who has known the mind of the Lord
    that he may instruct him?"
But we have the mind of Christ.

Holy Spirit and Holy Scripture

There is a heavy emphasis in 1 Corinthians 2:6-16 on the person and ministry of the Holy Spirit. Directly or indirectly he is mentioned nine or ten times. And the particular focus is on his teaching role. Indeed, this is a very important New Testament passage on the relations between the Spirit and the Word, between Holy Scripture and Holy Spirit. Christian leaders need to be clear on this topic.

Christians know that the Holy Spirit and the Holy Scriptures are supposed to have something to do with one another, and indeed Holy Scripture is the creative product of the Holy Spirit. As the Nicene Creed declares, "He spoke through the prophets." And as Peter affirmed, "Men spoke from God as they were carried along by the Holy Spirit" (2 Pet 1:21). It is the precise relationship between the Spirit and the Word that we are going to investigate in this chapter, and notably the part played by the Holy Spirit in the composition of the Scriptures. But first we must see the text in its context. Commentators agree that with 1 Corinthians 2:6 Paul's argument changes course. Up to this point he has been emphasizing the foolishness of the gospel of Christ crucified (1:18, 23). But now in verse 6 he writes, *We do, however, speak a message of wisdom among the mature.*

What does he mean? Gordon Fee, for example, argues forcefully that *God's secret wisdom* (v. 7) is the same as in chapter 1 and denotes the gospel of "salvation through a crucified Messiah," and that the mature *(teleioi)* are simply Christians whom God has called, not a special group.[1] Similarly, Donald Carson writes that "all Christians are mature in the sense that they have come to terms with the message of the cross."[2]

It is easy to understand the motives that impel commentators in this direction. They are anxious (and rightly so) to avoid any hint that there are two gospels, "a simple gospel of the cross for babes . . . and a different wisdom gospel for the mature,"[3] or that there are two classes of Christian, the initiated and the un-initiated. No, no! They rightly insist that there is only one gospel, the message of Christ crucified, and that all Christians may become mature; there is no esoteric grouping.

What does Paul mean, then, in verse 6? F. F. Bruce clarifies it. The wisdom Paul now says he spoke among the mature is "not something additional to the saving message of Christ crucified; it is in Christ crucified that the wisdom of God is embodied. It consists rather in the more detailed unfolding of the divine purpose summed up in Christ crucified."[4]

Thus, according to Bruce, although Paul does speak wisdom, he immediately adds three correctives or qualifications.

- It is wisdom *among* (i.e., for) *the mature*. It is not for the unregenerate. It is not even for babes in Christ, since it is "solid food" which they cannot digest (3:1-2). It is rather for mature Christians who are anxious to penetrate into the fullness of God's saving purpose through the cross.
- It is wisdom *from God* (2:7). It is *not the wisdom of this age or of the rulers of this age, who are coming to nothing* (v. 6). Nor is it "the wisdom of the wise" (1:19) or "the wisdom of the world" (1:20); it is "the wisdom of God" (1:21, 24; cf. 2:7).
- It is wisdom *destined for our glory* (*doxa*, 2:7). Now *doxa* is essentially an eschatological word: "We rejoice in the hope of the glory of God" (Rom 5:2). It includes the resurrection

body, which will be a body of glory (1 Cor 15:43; Phil 3:21), and the renewal of the universe (Rom 8:18-25, 30; 2 Cor 4:17). So God's wisdom for the mature is not just the good news of justification: it relates to our glorification as well. It alludes to the regeneration of all things through sharing in the glory of God. It concerns *what God has prepared for those who love him* (1 Cor 2:9).

All this seems to mean that there is a legitimate distinction between evangelism and Christian nurture. In evangelism we proclaim the foolishness of Christ crucified, which is the wisdom of God. We resolve to know nothing else, and through the folly of this message God saves those who believe. In Christian nurture, however—building people up into maturity—we do not leave the cross behind. Far from it. We rather teach the full implications of the cross, including our ultimate glorification. This is God's secret wisdom, which can be known only by revelation. It cannot be deduced by secular leaders. If they had known it, *they would not have crucified the Lord of glory* (1 Cor 2:8). They were not exceptional, however. All human beings, if left to themselves, are ignorant of God's will and purpose.

Paul insists on this in verse 9, which is a loose quotation of Isaiah 64:4. God's wisdom is something *no eye has seen* (it is invisible), *no ear has heard* (it is inaudible), and *no mind has conceived* (it is inconceivable). It is altogether beyond the reach of human eyes, ears and minds. It cannot be grasped either by scientific investigation or by poetic imagination. It is absolutely unattainable by our little, finite, fallen and fallible minds. It can be known only if God should choose to make it known—which is exactly what he has done: *God has revealed it to us by his Spirit* (1 Cor 2:10).

Thus Paul affirms most forcefully the necessity of revelation.

He is not denigrating our minds. He is simply insisting that the human mind, capable as it is of remarkable achievements in the empirical sciences, flounders helplessly out of its depth when it is seeking God.

The Old Testament equivalent to 1 Corinthians 2:9-10 is Isaiah 55:8-9, in which God says:

> "For my thoughts are not your thoughts,
>   neither are your ways my ways,"
>   declares the LORD.
> "As the heavens are higher than the earth,
>   so are my ways higher than your ways
>   and my thoughts than your thoughts."

In other words, the mind of God is as much higher than our minds as the heavens are higher than the earth, which is infinity. There is no ladder by which we can climb into the infinite mind of God. So how can we know his mind? The answer is that we cannot if he remains silent. Why, we cannot even read one another's minds. Try! What am I thinking about as I stop writing?

I'll tell you. I was picturing myself climbing the steeple of All Souls Church in London. But you had no idea what was going on in my mind. Now, however, you know exactly what I am thinking because I have resumed writing, and I am clothing the thoughts of my mind with the words of my mouth. If, then, we cannot read human minds unless we speak or write, how much less can we read God's mind unless he speaks or writes?

But God has spoken!

> As the rain and the snow
>   come down from heaven,

and do not return to it
  without watering the earth
and making it bud and flourish . . .
so is my word that goes out from my mouth:
  It will not return to me empty,
but will accomplish what I desire
  and achieve the purpose for which I sent it. (Is 55:10-11)

Similarly, *God has revealed it to us by his Spirit* (1 Cor 2:10). The word *us* is emphatic in the Greek sentence. It cannot refer to all Christian people, for we are not all recipients of direct divine revelation. It must rather refer to the apostles, to Paul himself and by extension to his fellow apostles. Another plural of apostolic authority occurs later in this letter: "Whether . . . it was I [Paul] or they [the other apostles], this is what we [all the apostles] preach, and this is what you believed' (15:11).

One is reminded also of Ephesians 3:4-5, where "the mystery of Christ," including the incorporation of Jews and Gentiles into his body on equal terms, "has now been revealed by the Spirit to God's holy apostles and prophets," who are also said to be the foundation on which the church is built (Eph 2:20). In both 1 Corinthians 2:10 and Ephesians 3:4-5, God is the author of the revelation, the Spirit is its agent, and the apostles are its recipients.

This, then, is the context. In what follows Paul gives us a comprehensive statement of the ministry of the Holy Spirit as the agent of the divine revelation. He is presented to us in four stages as "searching," "revealing," "inspiring" and "enlightening." Together these four verbs sum up the relations between the Holy Spirit and the Holy Scriptures.

STAGE 1: THE HOLY SPIRIT IS
THE SEARCHING SPIRIT (2:10-11)

Notice how this first verb assumes that the Holy Spirit is personal, for only persons with minds are capable of engaging in search and research. True, computers can analyze the data fed into them, but original research, as every doctoral student knows, requires personal investigation and reflection. This the Holy Spirit does because he is a person and has a mind of his own with which to think.

Paul now uses two fascinating pictures to indicate the Holy Spirit's unique qualifications in the work of divine revelation. He searches the depths and knows the thoughts of God.

First, *the Holy Spirit searches all things, even the deep things of God* (v. 10). The verb *eraunaō*, meaning "to investigate," is the one Jesus applied to the Jews who "searched" the Scriptures, studying them diligently (John 5:39). And Moulton and Milligan in their *Vocabulary of the Greek Testament* (1930) quote a papyrus from the third century A.D., in which the "searchers" seem to be customs officials who rummage about in travelers' baggage.

Further, *ta bathē* ("the depths") became in the second century A.D. a favorite term of the Gnostic heretics, who claimed to have been initiated into the depths of God. It may be an anachronism to suggest this here, but it is at least possible that Paul deliberately borrowed from their vocabulary, at the same time insisting that the deep things of God—"the depths of God's own self," even "God's inmost heart"[5]—were investigated and known not by proto-Gnostics but by the Holy Spirit himself. At all events, the Holy Spirit is depicted as a restlessly inquisitive researcher, even a deep-sea diver seeking to fathom the deepest

depths of the being of God. The Holy Spirit is God exploring
the infinity of God.

Second, the Holy Spirit *knows the thoughts of God* (v. 11). For
*who among men knows the thoughts of a man except the man's spirit
within him? In the same way no-one knows the thoughts of God except
the Spirit of God.* "Thoughts" is more literally "things," a human
being's things, perhaps our "humanness." Nobody understands
humanness except humans. An ant cannot possibly even begin
to conceive what it is like to be a human being. Nor can a frog or
a rabbit, or even a chimpanzee, for all its rich DNA. How often,
especially in adolescence, we complain, "Nobody understands
me!" It's true! Nobody understands me except I myself, and even
my own self-understanding is limited. Yet to some degree at least
human beings are self-conscious and self-aware.

Paul applies this concept of self-understanding to the Holy
Spirit, drawing a parallel: *In the same way,* he writes, *no one
knows the thoughts of God except the Spirit of God.* The Holy Spirit
is likened to the divine self-consciousness and self-understanding. Just as nobody can understand a human being except that
human being, so nobody can understand God except God himself. Only God knows God.

So then, to sum up this first truth about the Holy Spirit, he
searches the depths of God and knows the things of God. Both
statements indicate that the Holy Spirit has a unique understanding of God because he is himself God. This prompts the
question: What has the Holy Spirit done with what he has
searched out and come to know? Answer: He has done what
only he is competent to do—he has revealed it. Since only he
knows God, only he can make him known. The searching Spirit
becomes the revealing Spirit.

STAGE 2. THE HOLY SPIRIT IS
THE REVEALING SPIRIT (2:10, 12)

The Holy Spirit's work of revelation has already been stated in verse 10: *God has revealed it to us by his Spirit.* Now Paul elaborates this in verse 12: *We* (the same emphatic apostolic "we" as the "us" in verse 10) *have not received the Spirit of the world but the Spirit who is from God*—namely, the searching and knowing Spirit—*that we may understand what God has freely given us.*

This indicates that the apostles had received two separate but related gifts of God. First, they had received God's salvation, that is, what God has freely by grace given us. Second, they had received God's Spirit to enable them to understand the salvation he had freely given them.

The apostle Paul himself is perhaps the best example of this double divine gift, the gift of salvation and the gift of the Spirit. Paul's letters give us a superb exposition of the gospel of grace—how God set his love on the very people who did not deserve it; how he sent his Son to die for sinners like us who deserved nothing at his hand but judgment; how God raised him from the dead to demonstrate that he had not died in vain; and how, by faith inwardly and by baptism outwardly, we may become united to Christ in his death and resurrection. Paul's moving exposition stretches the mind and fires the heart. But how did he understand all this? How could he make such a comprehensive statement of salvation? The first answer is that he had himself received this salvation, while the second is that he had also received the Holy Spirit to interpret his experience to him. Thus the searching Spirit became the revealing Spirit, making God and his work of salvation known to the biblical authors.

STAGE 3: THE HOLY SPIRIT IS
THE INSPIRING SPIRIT (2:13)

This is what we speak or "we impart this" (RSV): namely, this understanding, which the apostles had been given by revelation. Verse 12 refers to what the apostles *received*, while verse 13 refers to what they went on to impart or *speak* to others. For the apostles imparted to others the understanding they had themselves received. Thus the searching Spirit, who had revealed God's plan of salvation *to* the apostles, went on to communicate it *through* them to others.

Just as the Spirit did not keep his research to himself but revealed it to the apostles, so the apostles in their turn did not keep his revelation to themselves but imparted or communicated it to others. They knew that they were trustees or stewards of God's revelation. They could not claim a monopoly of God's truth or keep it to themselves. No, truth is for sharing. So they delivered faithfully to others what they had themselves received. And how did they do so? Verse 13 answers: *not in words taught us by human wisdom but in words taught by the Spirit.*

Observe this further reference to the Holy Spirit. The same Spirit who searches the depths of God and who revealed God's secrets to the apostles now gave them the words with which to pass on this revelation to others. This is an unambiguous claim on the part of the apostle Paul to "verbal inspiration." That is, the very words in which the apostles expressed their message had been given them by the Holy Spirit.

Now the verbal inspiration of Scripture is an unpopular concept in the church today. But I strongly suspect that the reason it is unpopular is that it is misunderstood. So let me try to clarify what it means by three negatives (what it is not) and a single positive (what it is).

Verbal inspiration does not mean that "every word of the Bible is literally true" (a dictionary definition). The adverb *literally* is inappropriate, for the biblical authors have used a rich diversity of literary genres, each of which must be interpreted according to its own rules—history as history, parable as parable, poetry as poetry, and so on. What is inspired is the *natural* sense of the words, according to the intention of each author. For instance, when the author of Psalm 19 within a single verse likens the sun to a tent-dweller, a bridegroom and an athlete, we know that he is writing poetry, not science. Jesus himself sometimes used dramatic figures of speech in his teaching and rebuked his contemporaries for their excessive biblical literalism, as when Nicodemus thought the new birth was a second physical birth, and the Samaritan woman asked how Jesus could give her living water, since he did not have a bucket and the well was deep.

Verbal inspiration does not mean verbal dictation. The Christian understanding of the Bible is different from the Muslim understanding of the Qur'an. Muslims believe that Allah, through the medium of the angel Gabriel, dictated the Qur'an to Muhammad in Arabic, and that Muhammad had nothing to do except to take down the dictation. Christians, however, believe that the biblical authors were persons, not recording machines, and were in full possession of their faculties even while the Holy Spirit was communicating to them and through them. The phenomena of Scripture make this plain.

Thus each biblical author had his own vocabulary, literary style and theological emphasis. These distinctives of theirs were not ironed out by the process of inspiration. In addition, many biblical authors were historians, and much of the Bible is history. We do not imagine that all this history was supernaturally revealed to them. No, the human authors engaged in historical research, which is what Luke tells us he did (Lk 1:1-4). So divine inspiration and historical research are not incompatible. The inspiring Spirit did not smother the personality of the human authors. Their literary styles, theological emphases and historical research all demonstrate this.

Verbal inspiration does not mean that every text of Scripture is true even in isolation from its context. The Lausanne Covenant (1974) declares Scripture "without error in all that it affirms." But full weight must be given to this qualification, since not everything contained in the Bible is affirmed by the Bible.

Consider those long and tedious speeches by Job's so-called comforters. Their thesis, repeated *ad nauseam*, was that Job was being punished for his sins. But they were mistaken, as the context makes plain. In the first verse of the book Job is introduced as a righteous man, blameless and upright, who "feared God and shunned evil" (Job 1:1). And in the last chapter God twice says to the comforters that they have not spoken of him what was right (42:7, 8). We have no liberty, therefore, to quote any sentence from their speeches as God's word. It may not be. It may have been included in order to be contradicted, not endorsed. The book of Job as a whole is the Word of God, but each biblical text must be interpreted in its context.

After these three negatives, we can now be positive.

Verbal inspiration means that what the Holy Spirit spoke through the biblical authors (understood according to its literary genre, its plain, natural meaning, the intention of the human author and each context) is true and without error. There is no need to be embarrassed by, or afraid of, this traditional Christian belief. It is eminently reasonable because words are the building-blocks of sentences and so of speech. Words matter! Some theologians argue that what is inspired is the sense, not the words. But this is an unhelpful distinction because the sense depends on the words. It is impossible to convey a precise message without choosing precise words, as authors and speakers know. In the middle of the nineteenth century Charles Kingsley, the Christian socialist and prodigious author, wrote:

> These glorious things—words—are man's right alone. . . . Without words we should know no more of each other's hearts and thoughts than the dog knows of his fellow dog. For, if you will consider, you always think to yourself in words, though you do not speak them aloud; and without them all our thoughts would be mere blind longings,— feelings which we could not understand ourselves.

This, then, is the apostolic claim: the same Holy Spirit of God, who searches the depths of God and knows the thoughts of God, and who revealed his findings to the apostles, went on to communicate them to others through the apostles in words which he gave them. He spoke his words through their words, so that their words were simultaneously his. This is the double authorship of Scripture and the meaning of inspiration.

STAGE 4: THE HOLY SPIRIT IS THE ENLIGHTENING SPIRIT (2:13-16)

How are we to think of those who received the apostles' letters and listened to them being read? Were they left to themselves to understand what was written? Indeed not! The same Holy Spirit who was active in the apostles who wrote the letters was also active in those who received and read them. The Holy Spirit was working at both ends of the communication process—inspiring the apostles and enlightening their hearers and readers.

This is already implied at the end of verse 13, which reads *pneumatikois pneumatika synkrinontes*. It is a complicated and even enigmatic phrase which has been variously interpreted. The NIV has *expressing spiritual truths in spiritual words*. It seems to me, however, that the verb *synkrinō*, which can mean "combine," means here (as it usually does in the Septuagint) "to interpret" or "to explain." Then I think the RSV is correct in its rendering "interpreting spiritual truths to those who possess the Spirit."

In other words, the possession of the Holy Spirit is not limited to the biblical authors. Bible readers share in him too. To be sure, the Spirit's work of inspiration was unique. Preachers and teachers must not claim to be "inspired" as the apostles were. But to this unique apostolic experience the Spirit added his work of illumination and interpretation, which all Christians may experience.

It will be helpful if we distinguish between these words. *Revelation* and *inspiration* describe the unique, objective process by which the Holy Spirit taught the biblical authors. *Illumination,* however, describes the Holy Spirit's subjective work of enlightening our minds to grasp what they wrote. Supposing you were to bring a blindfolded friend to an unveiling ceremony, two actions would be necessary before your friend could read the words on the plaque. First, the plaque would have to be unveiled (which is revelation). Second, your friend's blindfold would need to be removed (which is illumination).

Verses 14 and 15 elaborate this truth and are in sharp contrast to each other. Verse 14 begins with a reference to the *psychikos,* the "natural" or unregenerate person, the *man without the Spirit.* Verse 15 begins, however, with a reference to the *spiritual man,* the person who has been born of the Spirit and consequently has the Spirit. For the indwelling of the Holy Spirit is the distinguishing mark of the true Christian: "If anyone does not have the Spirit of Christ, he does not belong to Christ' (Rom 8:9).

But what difference does it make whether we have the Holy Spirit or not? It makes all the difference in the world, not least in regard to our understanding. Look at verses 14 and 15 again.

The man without the Spirit (the *psychikos* person) *does not accept the things that come from the Spirit of God, for they are foolishness to him, and he cannot understand them, because they are spiritually discerned,* that is, discerned only with the aid of the enlightening Spirit.

The spiritual man (the *pneumatikos* person, who has the Spirit), by contrast, *makes judgments about all things,* or perhaps "discerns" all things (the verb is *anachrinoō,* as in the previous verse) or "evaluates" all things. He has not, of course, become omniscient or infallible, but things to which he was spiritually blind now at last begin to make sense to him. He understands what he had not understood before, even though he himself is not understood (the verb is *anachrinoō* for the third time) by anyone. That is, he remains something of an enigma to other people because of the inner secret of his spiritual life, which they have not experienced.

This is not surprising, because (Paul alludes to Isaiah 40:13) nobody knows the mind of the Lord or can interpret or instruct him. And since they cannot understand Christ's mind, they cannot understand ours either, who dare to say (because the Spirit enlightens us) that "we have the mind of Christ" (1 Cor 2:16).

This illumination of our minds by the Holy Spirit is common Christian experience. A good example is that of William Grimshaw, an eighteenth-century evangelical leader in England. After his conversion it was said of him, "If God had drawn up his Bible to heaven, and sent him down another, it could not have been newer to him."[6] I could say the same thing.

A digression seems to be needed at this point, in response to the following question, which may have formed in my readers' minds: "If the Holy Spirit is the enlightening Spirit, and if we have the mind of Christ, why is it that we still disagree with one another?" My general answer is that we actually agree with one another a great deal more than we disagree, and that we would agree more still if we fulfilled the following five conditions.

1. We must accept the supreme authority of Scripture. The big and painful Christian divisions are between the so-called reformed and unreformed churches, that is, between those churches which are determined to submit to Scripture and those which are unwilling to do so or which elevate traditions and opinions to the same level as Scripture. Among churches that do submit to the supremacy of Scripture we are perhaps 90 percent agreed.

2. We must remember that the chief purpose of Scripture is to bear witness to Jesus Christ as the Savior of sinners. In the central truths concerning Christ and salvation, Scripture is plain or "perspicuous." It is in the realm of the *adiaphora*, matters indifferent because of secondary importance, that we must give one another liberty of belief.

3. We must develop sound principles of biblical interpretation. It is often said that "you can make the Bible teach anything you like." I reply, "Yes, you are right, you can make the Bible teach anything, but only if you are unscrupulous enough." If we apply proper principles of interpretation to Scripture, we find that far from our manipulating it, it controls us. In particular, we must learn to look for the natural sense (whether literal or figurative), the original sense (as the author intended and his readers would have understood him) and the general sense (in harmony with the rest).

4. We must study Scripture together. The church is the hermeneutical community, in which God means his Word to be received and interpreted. We can help one another to understand it, especially if we reflect on it crossculturally. This is what Paul meant when he prayed that we might be able "with all the saints" to grasp the full dimensions of God's love (Eph 3:18). We could never do this alone. We need one another.

5. We must come to the biblical text with humble, open, receptive spirits. We must be ready for God to break through our cultural defenses, to challenge and to change us. If we come to Scripture with our minds made up and closed, we will never hear the thunderclap of his Word. All we will hear is what we want to hear, the soothing echoes of our own cultural prejudice.

The spiritual discernment the Holy Spirit promises to the students of Scripture is not given in defiance of these five conditions; it rather presupposes them.

CONCLUSION

We have considered the teaching role of the Holy Spirit in four stages—searching, revealing, inspiring and enlightening. First, he searches the depths of God and knows the thoughts of God, and is therefore uniquely qualified for his teaching role. Second, he revealed his findings to the apostles and the other biblical authors. Third, he communicated those things through the biblical authors to others and did so in words chosen by him. Fourth, he enlightens the minds of Bible readers to discern what he has revealed to and through the biblical authors, and continues this work of illumination today.

So we need to humble ourselves before both the Word and the Spirit. We still have to study the Word, to ponder its meaning and application, but we also need to cry to the Holy Spirit for enlightenment. Humble prayer and diligent study need to be combined. A heavenly messenger said to Daniel, "Since the first day that you set your mind to gain understanding and to humble yourself before your God, your words were heard" (Dan 10:12). Similarly Paul wrote to Timothy, "Reflect on what I am saying, for the Lord will give you insight into all this" (2 Tim 2:7). We do the pondering; he does the enlightening. For the Word remains a dead letter until the Spirit brings it to life.

Charles Simeon of Cambridge used to illustrate this point by reference to a sundial in the garden. If we consult the dial on a dull day, when the sun is not shining, we cannot tell the time. The dial has only figures; there is no message. But when the sun breaks through, and illumines the dial, immediately the finger points and we can tell the time.

Just so, if we read Scripture on a dull day, when there are clouds between us and God, the book has only paper and print;

there is no message. But when the clouds lift, and the sun breaks through, the light of the Spirit shines onto the printed page and into our minds, and God speaks through what he has spoken.

The Word and the Spirit belong to each other. Let's not separate what God has joined.

FOUR

The Church

and the Trinity

1 Corinthians 3

1 CORINTHIANS 3

Brothers, I could not address you as spiritual but as worldly—
mere infants in Christ. I gave you milk, not solid food, for you
were not yet ready for it. Indeed, you are still not ready. You
are still worldly. For since there is jealousy and quarrelling
among you, are you not worldly? Are you not acting like mere
men? For when one says, "I follow Paul," and another, "I follow
Apollos," are you not mere men?

What, after all, is Apollos? And what is Paul? Only servants,
through whom you came to believe—as the Lord has assigned
to each his task. I planted the seed, Apollos watered it, but God
made it grow. So neither he who plants nor he who waters is
anything, but only God, who makes things grow. The man who
plants and the man who waters have one purpose, and each
will be rewarded according to his own labor. For we are God's
fellow workers; you are God's field, God's building.

By the grace God has given me, I laid a foundation as an expert
builder, and someone else is building on it. But each one should

be careful how he builds. For no one can lay any foundation other than the one already laid, which is Jesus Christ. If any man builds on this foundation using gold, silver, costly stones, wood, hay or straw, his work will be shown for what it is, because the Day will bring it to light. It will be revealed with fire, and the fire will test the quality of each man's work. If what he has built survives, he will receive his reward. If it is burned up, he will suffer loss; he himself will be saved, but only as one escaping through the flames.

Don't you know that you yourselves are God's temple and that God's Spirit lives in you? If anyone destroys God's temple, God will destroy him; for God's temple is sacred, and you are that temple.

Do not deceive yourselves. If any one of you thinks he is wise by the standards of this age, he should become a "fool" so that he may become wise. For the wisdom of this world is foolishness in God's sight. As it is written: "He catches the wise in their craftiness"; and again, "The Lord knows that the thoughts of the wise are futile." So then, no more boasting about men! All things are yours, whether Paul or Apollos or Cephas or the world or life or death or the present or the future—all are yours, and you are of Christ, and Christ is of God.

The Church and the Trinity

The apostle reverts in 1 Corinthians 3 to the "divisions" (*schismata*) in the Corinthian church. In doing so, he attributes them partly to the sins of jealousy and quarrelling (v. 3) but especially to the Corinthians' fundamentally defective view of the church. Paul's thesis is this: If they had a true view of the church, they would have a true view of the leaders of the church. Indeed, if they had a *higher* view of the church, they would have a *lower* and more modest view of its leaders, for there would be *no more boasting about men* (v. 21).

1 Corinthians 3 is, in fact, one of the great New Testament chapters on the church. Evangelical people are sometimes criticized for being rugged individualists with a poverty-stricken and even nonexistent doctrine of the church. But if this were true, we would have departed from the biblical vision, including that of this chapter.

The connecting link between chapters 2 and 3 is clear. In 2:14 Paul insisted that spiritual truths can be discerned only by spiritual people. Now he tells the Corinthians bluntly that in his view they do not qualify as spiritual people. *Brothers*, he writes, *I could not address you as spiritual (**pneumatikoi**) but as worldly* (3:1). The last word of this sentence is an unfortunate NIV translation, because Paul's reference is not to the world (*kosmos*) but to the flesh (*sarx*), which is our fallen, self-centered and self-indulgent nature. In calling them "carnal" (*sarkinoi* or *sarkikoi*; the manuscripts vary), Paul is not suggesting that they are unregenerate. He does not call them *psychikoi*, the adjective used in

2:14 for those who do not possess the Spirit. Besides, he addresses them as *brothers*, members of God's family. So they are Christians, yet he indicates that they are not truly "spiritual" Christians, governed and controlled by the Holy Spirit. So he uses this third term *sarkinoi*. And he goes on to develop here the same antithesis between those who live according to the Spirit and those who live according to the flesh, with which we are familiar from Galatians 5 and Romans 8.

At the end of verse 1, Paul has a second way of saying the same thing. He now describes the Corinthians not only as "carnal" but as *mere infants in Christ. They have experienced new birth by the Spirit but have remained nēpioi*, babies in Christ; they have not yet become *teleioi*, mature in Christ. In Donald Carson's words, they are still "wretchedly, unacceptably, spiritually immature."[1] I fear that Paul would express the same opinion about many congregations today. We rejoice in the statistics of church growth, but it is often growth without depth. There is superficiality and immaturity everywhere.

On what grounds does the apostle make his evaluation of the Corinthian Christians, and lodge his complaint against them? By what criteria does he conclude that they are carnal, not spiritual; infantile, not mature? He tells us. The two main ways by which we can tell a child and its age are its diet and its behavior.

First, the child's diet. *I gave you milk, not solid food, for you were not yet ready for it. Indeed, you are still not ready* (v. 2). "One of the differences between milk and meat," a retired surgeon once pointed out to me, "is that milk is food already digested by another . . . one's mother or a cow or goat. Too often," he continued, "we want our food pre-digested by another," whereas the Lord wants us to digest his word ourselves.[2] Just as babies begin with milk—easily redigestible—and only gradually move on to solids, so Paul had been obliged to keep feeding the Corinthians with spiritual milk, or the rudiments of the gospel, because they were not yet ready for more solid instruction (cf. Heb 5:12-14; 1 Pet 2:2). That is, in spite of their knowledge, with which they had been enriched (1 Cor 1:5) and of which they boasted, they were still at an elementary stage in their Christian development—"a hard saying for the Corinthians," comments C. K. Barrett,[3] for they were very pleased with themselves.

What is the difference between spiritual meat and spiritual milk? Paul is certainly not saying that the cross is rudimentary teaching which we grow out of. No, "the difference between milk and strong meat . . . is simply the difference between the more or less perfect development of the things taught."[4] Similarly, "the argument of 2:6-16 implies that for Paul the gospel of the Crucified One is both 'milk' and 'solid food.' As milk it is the good news of salvation; as solid food it is understanding that the entire Christian life is predicated on the same reality."[5] We never grow out of the cross; we rather grow more deeply into it and into the fullness of its implications.

So the continuing need for spiritual milk is the first evidence that the Corinthians are still "babies" in Christ or, reverting to the earlier word, "carnal."

The second criterion by which maturity and immaturity can be assessed is the child's behavior. *For since there is jealousy and quarrelling among you, are you not worldly?* (v. 3). Here as in verse 1 the NIV rendering "worldly" is misleading. It should again be translated "carnal," remembering that both jealousy and quarrelling are included among "the works of the flesh" (Gal 5:19-20 KJV) or "the acts of the sinful nature." "So if you behave like this," Paul asks, "are you not carnal?" and *Are you not acting like mere men (**kata anthrōpon**) (1 Cor 3:3), following human instead of divine standards? For when one says, "I follow Paul," and another, "I follow Apollos," are you not mere men?* (v. 4)—that is, merely human rather than godly in your outlook?

Here, then, is Paul's threefold indictment of the Corinthian Christians. Their behavior was carnal, not spiritual (controlled by their fallen nature instead of by the Holy Spirit); babyish, not mature (suffering from what Freud called "infantile regression," reverting to babyhood, having never grown up); and human, not divine (their mindset being not godly but ungodly). And the evidence for this carnality, immaturity and ungodliness was partly their doctrinal diet (spiritual milk) and partly their moral failures (jealousy and quarrelling).

All this is of great concern to Christian leaders today, especially to those who have pastoral responsibilities in the local church. It would be hard to find a more appropriate or challenging goal than Paul's: "We proclaim him [Christ], admonishing and teaching everyone with all wisdom, so that we may present everyone perfect [*teleios*, better 'mature'] in Christ. To this end I labor, struggling with all his energy, which so powerfully works in me" (Col 1:28-29). We think of Paul as an evangelist, a missionary, a church-planter. But here he thinks of himself as a pastor, resolved above all else to lead his converts into Christian maturity.

The apostle now delves more deeply. He argues that the Corinthians have a defective understanding of the church, or they would never behave as they are doing. He develops three pictures or images of the church, each of which has important implications.

- The first is an agricultural metaphor: *God's field* (v. 9).
- The second is an architectural metaphor: *God's building* (v. 9).
- The third is an ecclesiastical metaphor: *God's temple* (v. 16).

1. YOU ARE GOD'S FIELD (3:5-9)

Paul asks two indignant questions in verse 5 to begin this thought: *What, after all, is Apollos? And what is Paul?* Note that he does not use the masculine gender and ask politely, "Who?" He deliberately uses the neuter. As J. B. Lightfoot wrote, the neuter is "much more emphatic" than the masculine: "it expresses greater disdain."[6]

Now see how he replies to his own questions as to who he and Apollos are: *Only servants, through whom you came to believe* (v. 5). That is, Paul and Apollos are not masters to whom the Corinthians owed allegiance but servants—only servants. Moreover, they are not servants *in* whom the Corinthians had believed, for they are not the objects of their faith. Neither are they servants *from* whom the Corinthians had believed, for they were not the authors of their faith. But they are servants *through* whom the Corinthians had come to believe (agents or instruments through whom God had worked to elicit their faith). Further, this came about *as the Lord has assigned to each his task.*

All three parts of verse 5 are designed to demote, even debunk, the leaderswhom the Corinthians are improperly elevating.

- These leaders are only things (in the neuter), instruments of divine activity.
- They are only servants, agents through whom God had worked.
- They are only doing the job that has been assigned to them by the Lord.

So neither the Corinthians nor their leaders have anything to boast about.

In verses 6-8 the apostle identifies the different tasks that have to be done in the church, illustrating them from his agricultural metaphor and applying them to himself and Apollos. There are three main tasks to be done if a field is to produce a harvest, namely planting the seed, watering the seed, and causing the seed to sprout; or sowing, irrigation and growth. Paul applies this to Corinth historically or chronologically in verse 6.

- First, *I planted the seed*. That is, Paul reached Corinth first, during his second missionary journey, and evangelized the city (see Acts 18:1-18).

- Next, *Apollos watered it*. He followed Paul to Corinth. Luke recounts the story in Acts 18:24-26. These two men accomplished their pioneer tasks in relation to the seed.

- *But God made it grow*.

The tenses of the three verbs in verse 6 enforce Paul's point. "I planted" is an aorist verb. Paul came to Corinth, proclaimed the gospel, planted the church and moved on. Then along came Apollos and watered the seed (another aorist verb), and went on his way. But "God made it grow" is an imperfect verb, since all the time—incessantly—through the ministries of both Paul and Apollos, God was giving growth to the seed.

In verse 7 Paul compares with one another the three actors involved in the evangelization of Corinth and the establishment of its church, namely, himself, Apollos and God. *So neither he who plants nor he who waters is anything*. Both planting and watering are unskilled and somewhat mechanical jobs. Anybody can do them. It requires no professional expertise to drop seeds into soil or to sprinkle water on the seeds sown. A Ph.D. is not necessary. No, what really counts and is indispensable is the mysterious third stage, namely, causing the seed to sprout and bear fruit. No human being can do this. Paul could not do it with all his apostolic authority. Apollos could not do it with all his knowledge of the Scriptures and his famous eloquence. It is *only God, who makes things grow.*

Paul adds a further point in verses 8-9 which demonstrates the stupidity of the Corinthians' behavior. So far he has stressed that planters and waterers count for nothing in themselves; so it is foolish to exalt their ministries. Now he points out that both *the man who plants and the man who waters have one purpose* (v. 8). Their different tasks serve the same goal, namely, to secure a good harvest. So it is silly to set them in competition with each other. Further, *each will be rewarded according to his own labor* (v. 8). God will do this on judgment day. So it is senseless of the Corinthians to try to anticipate that day by promoting different personalities. *For,* he concludes, *we are God's fellow workers,* and *you are God's field* (v. 9).

We need to interpret this assertion in its context. Since the aim of the whole passage is to downplay the role exercised by human leaders, it is unlikely that the sentence means "We have the privilege of working with God," although to be sure this is taught elsewhere. Here Paul seems to be saying not "We are partners with God" but rather "We are fellow workers [with each other] in God's service" (Revised English Bible).

What lesson are we intended to learn from this first metaphor? The imagery of the field (the planting, the watering and the giving of growth) does not teach everything we want to know about Christian leadership and ministry. It is always dangerous to push an analogy beyond the point at which it is being drawn. It is always unwise to argue from an analogy, saying that because the church is a field, everything about fields has a parallel in the church. Instead, we have to ask at what point the analogy is being drawn.

The metaphor of the field says nothing about gifts in distinction to roles and offices, and nothing about the honor attached to being an evangelist, missionary or pastor. For these things we need to look elsewhere in the New Testament. Instead, like most metaphors it is intended to highlight one main point, namely that in God's field (the church) it is God's activity that really matters. God allocates the tasks. God gives the growth. God rewards the laborers.

So we must give glory not to ourselves as leaders or to our fellow workers but to God the Lord alone. The church would be a happier and more harmonious community if we remembered this principle.

2. YOU ARE GOD'S BUILDING (3:9-16)

The apostle moves on at the end of verse 9 from his agricultural metaphor (*you are God's field*) to his architectural metaphor (*you are God's building*). Yet both illustrate what it means to be *God's fellow workers*, that is, collaborators in the service of God. For whether we are cultivating a field or constructing a building, we are a team of farmers or builders, working together and not laboring on our own, serving a common enterprise, pursuing a common goal.

Just as in God's field one plants and another waters, so on God's building one lays the foundation while another erects the superstructure. Yet the two metaphors do not make precisely the same point. The emphasis in God's field is that only God gives the growth, while the emphasis in God's building is that only Christ is its foundation, indeed only Christ crucified.

Again Paul applies the metaphor to himself and other leaders. *By the grace God has given me* (an expression he uses at least five times in his letters to refer to his commissioning as an apostle of Jesus Christ; see Rom 1:5; 12:3; 1 Cor 15:10; Gal 2:9; Eph 3:7-8), *I laid a foundation as an expert builder* (1 Cor 3:10). "Expert" translates *sophos,* "wise." Perhaps Paul is again saying that the true wisdom is in Christ. Certainly Paul had been given the pioneering task of preaching Christ crucified in Corinth (2:2). He goes on: *and someone else is building on it.* He makes no mention of Apollos by name, for several teachers had followed Paul, good and bad, true and false.

Paul's main point is to sound a warning to all Christian teachers in regard both to the foundation they lay and to the superstructure they erect on it: *each one should be careful how he builds* (1 Cor 3:10). What kind of "carefulness" does he have in mind?

The foundation. Builders should not tamper with a house's foundation once it has been laid, trying to dig it up or relay it. *For no one can lay any foundation other than the one already laid, which is Jesus Christ* (v. 11). This is the foundation Paul had laid (v. 10). As we love to sing, "The church's one foundation is Jesus Christ her Lord," and this is not another Jesus (cf. 2 Cor 11:4) but the Jesus of the apostolic witness, who is the only authentic Jesus—namely, Jesus the crucified one. "Paul does not mean," writes C. K. Barrett, "that it would be impossible to construct a community on a different basis, only that such a community will not be the church."[7]

The superstructure. Builders also have to be very careful about the materials they use in erecting the superstructure.

Broadly speaking, there are only two possibilities. One is *gold, silver, costly stones* (probably marble). These are valuable and durable (cf. 1 Chron 29:2) and represent true Christian teaching that will stand the test of time and of the judgment day. The other possibility is *wood, hay or straw*. These are cheap, perishable materials and represent false teaching or the wisdom of the world. In both cases the quality of the materials used by the builders (i.e., the teachers) *will be shown for what it is, because the Day will bring it to light. It will be revealed with fire, and the fire will test the quality of each man's work* (1 Cor 3:12-13).

What will be the result of this trial by fire? Just as there are two possible materials, so there will be two results. On the one hand, if the builder's work is made of durable material (gold, silver, marble) it will survive, and *he will receive his reward* (v. 14). On the other hand, if his work is made of combustible materials (wood, hay, straw), it will be consumed. In this case *he will suffer loss*, and his teaching will be seen to be valueless. But in the mercy of God *he himself will be saved, but only as one escaping through the flames* (v. 15), or as we might say, "only by the skin of his teeth." He will lose his reward but not his salvation.

There is surely here no allusion to purgatory, as Roman Catholic commentators tend to argue. The reference is to teachers in particular and not to all believers, and the purpose of the fire is not to purify (as in purgatory) but to test and to judge. As T. C. Edwards writes, Paul "speaks of a probation, not of a purification."[8]

Paul issues a solemn warning here to all Christian teachers. The Christian teaching ministry is of the greatest importance because it is designed to build up the church. If what we teach is true, biblical and balanced, we shall be adding a valuable building to the foundation, and it will last. If, however, our teaching is unbiblical, the wisdom of the world, then we are adding a ramshackle superstructure that will not survive. Thus what we teach will bless or harm the church not only for time but even for eternity.

3. YOU ARE GOD'S TEMPLE (3:16-17)

First Corinthians 3:16-17 is an extension of Paul's architectural metaphor, since of course a temple is a building. But the apostle develops it differently, since he is thinking of one particular and religious building, the temple, indeed the inner sanctuary, which is what *naos* really means.

Don't you know that you yourselves are God's temple? Paul asks (v. 16). No fewer than ten times in this letter the apostle asks the same question, *Don't you know?* He attributes the Corinthians' failures to their ignorance or forgetfulness. If only they knew, they would behave differently. Paul sees Christian understanding as the key to Christian holiness, especially our understanding of our identity as the people of God.

In the Old Testament, the essence of the temple in Jerusalem, as of the tabernacle before it, is that it was the dwelling place of God. "I will dwell among them," God had said (Ex 25:8). He promised that the Shekinah glory, the visible symbol of his presence, would inhabit and illumine the Holy of Holies. And the major promise regarding the rebuilt temple was that "the name of the city. . . will be: THE LORD IS THERE" (Ezek 48:35).

In the New Testament, however, God's temple or dwelling place is his people. Now the individual Christian's body (1 Cor 6:19), now the local church (3:16) and now the universal church (including Gentiles) "are being built together to become a dwelling in which God lives by his Spirit" (Eph 2:22).

So in God's sanctuary today—namely, the church—there is neither an image (as in pagan temples) or a symbol (like the Shekinah glory in the Jerusalem temple) but the Holy Spirit of God himself (1 Cor 3:16). The sacred wonder of the church, therefore, is that it is the dwelling place of God by his Spirit. Of course, "church" means people, not buildings, and God's presence is tied not to buildings but to his covenant people, to whom he has pledged himself. Wherever they are, there he is also, especially when they assemble for worship, even in small numbers, for then he is there in their midst (Mt 18:20). He promises also to be with them when they go on their mission (28:20).

Because of the sacred nature of the Christian community as the dwelling place of God, it must not be dishonored in any way—divided by jealousies and rivalries, deceived by false teaching or defiled by immoral conduct. These things are acts of sacrilege; they effectively destroy the church, for they destroy its unique identity as the holy people of God indwelt by the Spirit of God. And *if anyone destroys God's temple, God will destroy him; for God's temple is sacred, and you are that temple* (1 Cor 3:17). This is a severe statement. But then to destroy the church (by dividing, deceiving or defiling it) is an extremely serious offense. So a deliberate act of violence against the church is an act against God. This surely shows that the perpetrator in mind is not a true believer. He will be destroyed in hell, for that is what *destruction* means in the New Testament.

We need to keep reminding ourselves that the church is God's sanctuary. It may (in our view) consist of uneducated, unclean, unattractive people. And the congregation may be small and, like the Corinthian church, immature and factious. Nevertheless, it is the church of God (1:2), his dwelling place by his Spirit, and needs to be treated as such. Looking back over this chapter so far, note Paul's threefold, indeed trinitarian portrayal of the church. It highlights the role of God (Father, Son and Holy Spirit) in relation to the church, and it thereby downplays the role of human beings, especially of leaders. What matters most about the church, Paul insists, is that as God's field its growth is caused by God himself, as God's building its only foundation is Jesus Christ, and as God's temple it is the dwelling place of the Holy Spirit. This is the apostle's comprehensive vision of the church. It owes its existence and growth to God the Father. It is built on the foundation of God the Son. It is indwelt by God the Holy Spirit. It is a unique, trinitarian community. There is no other community in the world that even remotely resembles it.

In verses 18-23 Paul wraps up his godly perspective on the church by a further reference to wisdom and folly. For the wisdom of God includes his new society. So if the Corinthian Christians belittle God's church by exalting human leaders, they are showing their folly, not their wisdom. *Do not deceive yourselves*, Paul writes. *If any one of you thinks he is wise by the standards of this age* (i.e., according to the prevailing wisdom of the world), *he should* be willing to *become a "fool"* (in the eyes of the world) *so that he may become* truly *wise* (v. 18). *For the wisdom of this world is foolishness in God's sight.* To clinch his argument Paul quotes two verses from the Old Testament wisdom literature, namely, Job 5:13 and Psalm 94:11. Both express God's rejection of worldly wisdom. *As it is written: "He catches the wise in their craftiness"* (v. 19), *and again, "The Lord knows that the thoughts of the wise are futile"* (v. 20).

What was needed, then? The Corinthians needed to repent of their boastful, self-centered human wisdom and to develop a new humility, summed up in the slogan *no more boasting about men!* (v. 21). This is the climax of the passage, although Paul goes on to finalize his thesis. Instead of taking pride in their leaders, and claiming to belong to them, the exact opposite was the case. *All things are yours* (v. 21), *whether Paul or Apollos or Cephas* (Peter; v. 22). That is to say, far from the Corinthians belonging to their leaders, if anybody belonged to anybody in the Christian community, their leaders belonged to them. The Corinthians were not to say, "I belong to Paul," or "I belong to Peter," for Paul and Peter were theirs.

More than that. Not only are your leaders yours, Paul continues, but *all things are yours,* including *the world or life or death or the present or the future.* It is an almost incredible statement, but the reason for it is plain. All things are ours because we are Christ's and Christ is God's (v. 23). As in Romans 8:17, we are "heirs of God and co-heirs with Christ." So what belongs to him belongs to us, if he is ours.

This question of who belongs to whom in the church is still a vital issue today. When I was ordained over fifty years ago, the accepted way to begin a letter to a bishop was "My Lord," while the accepted conclusion was "I am your lordship's obedient servant." I am glad that I managed to keep it up for only a year or two, and that this form of address has long since been discontinued. But it should never have been begun.

Similarly, I doubt if pastors and church elders are wise to use the possessive adjective in relation to the church and refer to "my church," "my people," "my congregation." They do not belong to us, nor do we have any proprietary rights over them. It would be entirely biblical for them to refer to us as their ministers. But when we speak of them, it would be more modest to allude to them as "the people we have been called to serve." For we are their servants; they are not ours.

CONCLUSION

We urgently need a healthy, biblical understanding of the church, for only then shall we have a healthy, biblical understanding of Christian leadership. We must not define the church in terms of its leaders but rather define leaders in relation to the church.

We must also renounce secular views of the church as a merely human institution like any other corporate body, with human leaders wielding human authority and being lionized as celebrities. All that has to go.

In their place we need to develop a godly view of the church as a unique community unlike any other: the redeemed and covenant people of God. In this community ministers give humble service. There is no boasting about human beings, but all boasting is directed to God the Holy Trinity: to God the Father, who alone gives growth to the seed, to God the Son, who alone is the foundation of the church, and to God the Holy Spirit, who alone indwells and sanctifies the church.

So "no more boasting about men!" (1 Cor 3:21), but "Let him who boasts boast in the Lord" (1:31).

FIVE

Models of Ministry

1 Corinthians 4

1 CORINTHIANS 4

So then, men ought to regard us as servants of Christ and as those entrusted with the secret things of God. Now it is required that those who have been given a trust must prove faithful. I care very little if I am judged by you or by any human court; indeed, I do not even judge myself. My conscience is clear, but that does not make me innocent. It is the Lord who judges me. Therefore judge nothing before the appointed time; wait till the Lord comes. He will bring to light what is hidden in darkness and will expose the motives of men's hearts. At that time each will receive his praise from God.

Now, brothers, I have applied these things to myself and Apollos for your benefit, so that you may learn from us the meaning of the saying, "Do not go beyond what is written." Then you will not take pride in one man over against another. For who makes you different from anyone else? What do you have that you did not receive? And if you did receive it, why do you boast as though you did not?

Already you have all you want! Already you have become rich! You have become kings—and that without us! How I wish that you really had become kings so that we might be kings with you! For it seems to me that God has put us apostles on display at the end of the procession, like men condemned to die in the arena. We have been made a spectacle to the whole universe, to angels as well as to men. We are fools for Christ, but you are so wise in Christ! We are weak, but you are strong! You are honored, we are dishonored! To this very hour we go hungry and thirsty, we are in rags, we are brutally treated, we are homeless. We work hard with our own hands. When we are cursed, we bless; when we are persecuted, we endure it; when we are slandered, we answer kindly. Up to this moment we have become the scum of the earth, the refuse of the world.

I am not writing this to shame you, but to warn you, as my dear children. Even though you have ten thousand guardians in Christ, you do not have many fathers, for in Christ Jesus I became your father through the gospel. Therefore I urge you to imitate me. For this reason I am sending to you Timothy, my son whom I love, who is faithful in the Lord. He will remind you of my way of life in Christ Jesus, which agrees with what I teach everywhere in every church.

Some of you have become arrogant, as if I were not coming to you. But I will come to you very soon, if the Lord is willing, and then I will find out not only how these arrogant people are talking, but what power they have. For the kingdom of God is not a matter of talk but of power. What do you prefer? Shall I come to you with a whip, or in love and with a gentle spirit?

Models of Ministry

There is much contemporary confusion about the nature of the ordained pastoral ministry. What are clergy? Are they primarily priests, presbyters, pastors, prophets, preachers or psychotherapists? Are they administrators, facilitators, managers, social workers, evangelists or liturgists? There are many options.

Yet this uncertainty is not new. Throughout its long and checkered history the church has oscillated between the opposite extremes of clericalism (which puts clergy on a pedestal) and anticlericalism (which knocks them off again and even declares them redundant). Now that many churches have recovered the Pauline vision of the "every-member-ministry" of the body of Christ, radical questions are being asked. Are clergy necessary any longer? Are they not superfluous? Wouldn't the church be healthier without them? Should we perhaps form a Society for the Abolition of the Clergy?

In Mark Twain's book *The Adventures of Huckleberry Finn* (1884), Huck gets into a conversation one day with Joanna, the youngest daughter of Peter Wilks, who has died. He tells her that in the church of the Rev. Harvey Wilks (her uncle from Shefield) there are "no less than seventeen clergy," although, he adds, "they don't *all* of 'em preach the same day—only *one* of 'em."

"Well, then, what does the rest of 'em do?"

"Oh, nothing much. Loll around, pass the plate—and one thing or another. But mainly they don't do nothing."

"Well, then," asks Joanna in wide-eyed astonishment, "what are they for?"

"Why, they're for style," Huck responds. "Don't you know nothing?"[1]

Actually, this confusion goes right back to the beginning. We recall the first-century Corinthian church, in which different factions were claiming the patronage of particular leaders, saying "I belong to Paul" or "I belong to Apollos" or "I belong to Peter." Paul is horrified by this personality cult. "What on earth do you think we are," he asks incredulously, speaking of the human leaders derogatorily in the neuter, "that you should pay such exaggerated deference to us?" (cf. 1 Cor 3:5).

And now in 1 Corinthians 4 the apostle proceeds to answer his own question. *So then, men ought to regard us as . . .* (v. 1) or "This is how one should regard us, as . . ." (RSV). He goes on to elaborate four essentials of authentic pastoral ministry. They describe in the first place Paul's own unique apostolic ministry, but in a secondary sense they also apply to all pastoral ministers today, especially when we remember Paul's injunction to the Corinthian leadership that they should imitate him (v. 16). He outlines four models of ministry.

1. PASTORS ARE THE SERVANTS OF CHRIST (4:1)

Before we can be ministers of the Word or ministers of the church, we must be ministers of Christ. Dr George Carey, Archbishop of Canterbury, has expressed this truth well. He has written that

> prior to everything to do with structures, management, policy and finance, is the bedrock of Christian assurance. For myself, . . . I remain convinced that above all else the [minister's] training must take the student more deeply and challengingly into relationship with Jesus.[2]

The word for *servants* here is not *diakonos* (as in 3:5) but *hypēretēs*. Robertson and Plummer write, "The word originally denoted those who row *(eressein)* in the lower tier of a trireme [an ancient Greek three-tiered warship], and then came to mean those who do anything under another, and hence simply 'underlings.'"[3] Nineteenth-century commentators followed this etymology, but it is questioned today. Tony Thiselton writes, "In classical Greek the word could mean *underrower* in appropriate contexts, but although Corinth was a seaport the addressees would probably not be expected to think primarily of this meaning."[4]

Of course, there are other New Testament texts that emphasize the nobility of the pastorate (e.g., 1 Tim 3:1) and call the church to hold its pastors in high esteem because of their work (e.g., 1 Thess 5:12-13). Nevertheless, Paul begins his account of his own ministry with a title not of honor and glory but of lowliness. "We are . . . Christ's subordinates" (Revised English Bible) or "underlings."

Fundamental to all Christian leadership and ministry is a humble personal relationship with the Lord Jesus Christ, devotion to him expressed in daily prayer and love for him expressed in daily obedience. Without this, Christian ministry is impossible. In addition to this, being Christ's subordinates, we are accountable to him for our service, for he is our Lord and our judge. This fact brings both comfort and challenge.

On the one hand, being Christ's servant is a very comforting thing. It enables us to say: *I care very little if I am judged by you or by any human court; indeed, I do not even judge myself* (1 Cor 4:3). Paul elaborates: *My conscience is clear* (literally, "I know nothing against myself"), *but* even a clear conscience *does not make me innocent. It is the Lord who judges me* (v. 4).

Having insisted that he is accountable for his ministry to the Lord Jesus Christ his judge, and not to any human judges (whether himself or others), he draws a practical conclusion: *Therefore judge nothing before the appointed time.* Premature judgments are always unwise. So *wait till the Lord comes,* for then everything will be made clear. *He will bring to light what is hidden in darkness and will expose the motives of men's hearts.* Nothing will be concealed from him. There will be no possibility of a miscarriage of justice. *At that time each will receive his praise* (or censure) *from God* (v. 5).

Paul is not enunciating a merely abstract principle, he adds. On the contrary, *I have applied these things* concretely or "as an object-lesson"[5] *to myself and Apollos for your benefit, so that you may learn from us the meaning of the saying, "Do not go beyond what is written,"* or do not go beyond Scripture. *Then you will not take pride in one man over against another* (v. 6), for Scripture continually humbles us and leaves us no room for boasting.

Paul brings these things home to the Corinthians by asking them a series of questions. First, *Who makes you different from anyone else?* The anticipated answer is that all distinctions between us come from God. Second, *What do you have that you did not receive?* Answer, nothing. Third, *If you did receive it, why do you boast as though you did not?* (v. 7). No intelligent answer is possible; all boasting is frankly absurd.

This whole passage (vv. 3-7) emphasizes one main point, namely, that ministers of Christ (whatever form their ministry may take) are accountable to Christ for their ministry. Of course, we must listen to human criticism, however painful it may be, especially if it is untrue, unfair or unkind. But ultimately we are responsible to Christ, and I believe him to be a more just and merciful judge than any human being, committee, council or synod.

This tells us what to do with anonymous letters. They can be very hurtful, but if the author of a letter lacks the courage to divulge his or her identity, we should not take its message too seriously. A story is told of Joseph Parker, who occupied the pulpit of the City Temple in London when C. H. Spurgeon was preaching in the Metropolitan Tabernacle. One day, when Parker was climbing the steps to his pulpit, a lady in the gallery threw a piece of paper at him. He picked it up and read it. It contained only one word: "Fool!" Parker began his sermon with these words: "I have received many anonymous letters in my life. Previously they have been a text without a signature. Today for the first time I have received a signature without a text!"

However, if on the one hand it is a comforting thing to be accountable to Christ, on the other it is challenging, for his standards are high and holy. And though much of a pastor's work is unseen and unsupervised by human beings, yet we are always in his presence. And we shall never grow slack or careless if we remember that he is watching us and that one day we shall have to give an account to him.

2. PASTORS ARE THE STEWARDS OF REVELATION (4:1-2)

Returning to 1 Corinthians 4, Paul advances from our general responsibility as Christ's "servants" to our more particular duty as his "stewards." True, the word for *steward* (*oikonomos*) does not occur in the text, but the concept is there. We are *those en-*

trusted with the secret things of God, or "stewards of the mysteries of God" (RSV).

God's "mysteries" are of course his revealed secrets. They are truths hitherto concealed but now revealed, truths known only by revelation. These revealed truths relate to Christ, his salvation and the incorporation of Jews and Gentiles on equal terms in the body of Christ. Of these revealed truths, now contained in the New Testament, the apostles were the original stewards or trustees (cf. 2:10). But Christian pastors today, albeit in a secondary sense, are also stewards of divine revelation. God has entrusted the Scriptures to us that we in our turn may expound them to others. It is not an accident that in Anglican churches worldwide newly ordained presbyters are given a Bible as the symbol of their office. This reminds us of three important facts.

First, pastors are essentially teachers. This is evident from the ten conditions of eligibility for the presbyterate that Paul lays down in 1 Timothy 3. Nine of them are moral or social (e.g., self-controlled, hospitable, sober, gentle). Only one could be called a "professional" qualification, namely, *didaktikos* (v. 2), "a good teacher" (Revised English Bible).

Second, what we teach has been entrusted to us in the Scriptures; it is not our responsibility to invent or compose our message.

Third, we are required above all else to be faithful: "Now stewards are required to show themselves trustworthy" (1 Cor 4:2 Revised English Bible). That is, having received a trust, and having been appointed trustees, we are expected to be trustworthy.

Yet it is very easy to be unfaithful stewards, and I fear that there are many such in the church today—now rejecting the authority of the Word of God, now neglecting to study it, now failing to relate it sensitively to the contemporary world, now manipulating it to mean what they want it to mean, now selecting from it what they like and discarding what they do not like, now even contradicting its plain meaning and substituting for it their own threadbare speculations, and now flagrantly disobeying it in their own lives.

No wonder in many places the church languishes! So let's resolve instead to be faithful, to develop disciplined habits of study, to study both the ancient Word and the modern world in order to relate the one to the other, never knowingly twisting or distorting or disobeying the teaching of Scripture.

Donald Coggan, a former archbishop of Canterbury, wrote two books about preaching. In one of them, in a chapter titled "The Preacher as Trustee," he writes:

> The Christian preacher has a boundary set for him. When he enters the pulpit he is not an entirely free man. There is a very real sense in which it may be said of him that the Almighty has set him his bounds that he shall not pass. He is not at liberty to invent or choose his message; it has been committed to him, and it is for him to declare, expound and commend it to his hearers. . . . It is a great thing to come under the magnificent tyranny of the Gospel.[6]

3. PASTORS ARE THE SCUM OF THE EARTH (4:8-13)

In 1 Corinthians 4:8-13 the apostle uses three vivid metaphors from the Greco-Roman world to illustrate his theme. First, he takes us to a public amphitheater in which criminals fight to the death. Second, we find ourselves in a kitchen in which the floor is being swept and pots are being scraped. Third, we visit a plague-ridden city in which scapegoats are sacrificed to the gods.

First, we are in an amphitheater on a public holiday. *For it seems to me*, Paul writes, *that God has put us apostles on display at the end of the procession, like men condemned to die in the arena* (v. 9). The theater is packed with excited crowds. Event follows event throughout the day. Then, as the grand finale, criminals are either thrown to the lions or forced to fight with gladiators. This is how Paul characterizes himself and his fellow apostles. *We have been made a spectacle to the whole universe, to angels as well as to men*, a bit of cosmic theater.

Paul is deliberately contrasting himself with the smug security and self-satisfaction of the Corinthian Christians. Look back to the previous verse: *Already*, he writes with more than a touch of sarcasm, *you have all you want! Already you have become rich! You have become kings—and that without us! How I wish that you really had become kings so that we might be kings with you!* (v. 8). Twice he uses the "already" of a realized eschatology. "These highly blessed Corinthians are already in the kingdom of God, enjoying its banquets, its treasures and its thrones. . . . They have got a private millennium of their own."[7] Everything for them is "already"; there is no corresponding "not yet." Already they are eating and drinking and reigning. Paul wishes he could join them in the celebration. But he knows that the path to glory is suffering. It was for Jesus; it is for his followers too. They have forgotten the cross. If the Corinthians are kings, the apostles are like criminals condemned to death.

Paul's second metaphor is that of the kitchen. At the end of verse 13 he uses two unusual words which have a somewhat similar meaning: *Up to this moment we have become the scum of the earth, the refuse of the world.* The first expression translates *perikatharmata.* Derived from *perikatheirō,* "to clean thoroughly," it seems to refer to sweepings off the floor. The second expression translates *peripsēma.* Derived from *peripsaō,* "to wipe clean," it seems to refer to scrapings from a dirty pot. Both allude to "the filth that one gets rid of through the sink or the gutter."[8]

In Paul's third picture we enter a Greek city stricken by some calamity like the plague. In order to appease the supposed anger of the pagan gods, some poor wretches are taken from the community, thrown into the sea and drowned. These scapegoats were called the dregs or scum of society. "That's what we are," writes Paul in effect (v. 13).

You will agree that these are extraordinary statements. Between verse 10 and verse 13 Paul explains. He is referring to his sufferings in contrast to Corinthian complacency. At the end of chapter 1 Paul argued that socially they were weak and foolish when God called them (1:26-29). Now he reverses the situation spiritually: *We are fools for Christ, but you are so wise in Christ! We are weak, but you are strong! You are honored, we are dishonored!* (4:10).

Next Paul describes some of his physical privations and persecutions. *To this very hour we go hungry and thirsty, we are in rags, we are brutally treated, we are homeless* (v. 11). *We work hard with our own hands* (v. 12). But Paul knows the teaching and example of Jesus; he does not retaliate. On the contrary, *when we are cursed, we bless; when we are persecuted, we endure it; when we are slandered, we answer kindly. Up to this moment we have become the scum of the earth, the refuse of the world* (vv. 12-13).

It all sounds very remote from us. Most readers of these pages are likely to have a good job, a nice home, plenty to eat and adequate clothing. In fact, the difficulty we have in applying this text to ourselves may indicate how far we have drifted from the New Testament. True, the persecution of Christians is increasing in some (especially Hindu and Muslim) cultures. Yet most of us are not cursed, persecuted or slandered. Today, even in a non-Christian, pluralist or secular culture it is still regarded as quite respectable, even honorable, to be ordained to the clergy. In some countries, clergy receive tax and travel concessions. And some people even murder the English language and call us "reverend!"

But it is not so everywhere, and it should certainly not be taken for granted. I think we need to listen again to the words of Jesus: "Woe to you when all men speak well of you" (Lk 6:26). Beware, I beg you, of the temptation to be a popular preacher! I doubt if it is possible to be popular and faithful at the same time. Either we go for popularity at the expense of faithfulness, or we are determined to be faithful even at the expense of popularity. If we compromised less, we would undoubtedly suffer more. For the cross is still foolishness to some and a stumbling block to others. What is it, then, about the gospel that arouses people's opposition?

First, the gospel offers eternal life as a free gift. But we are such proud creatures that we don't want a free gift. We would do anything to be able to earn our salvation, or at least to contribute to it. To be told that we cannot is almost unbearably humiliating.

Second, the gospel declares that Jesus Christ is the only Savior. He is unique in his incarnation, his atonement and his resurrection. Nobody else possesses these qualifications. But in our increasingly pluralistic age our emphasis on the uniqueness, the finality and the exclusiveness of Jesus is deeply offensive to people.

Third, the gospel demands holiness as the evidence of salvation. If only Jesus would oblige us by lowering his moral standards! But no, he calls us to surrender to his lordship.

Here are three stumbling blocks—the freeness, the exclusiveness and the moral ethic of the gospel. They are different aspects of the stumbling block of the cross. Dietrich Bonhoeffer, the German Lutheran pastor who was hanged in April 1945 in the Flossenbürg concentration camp, had experienced suffering himself.

> *Suffering is the badge of the true Christian. The disciple is not above his master. . . . Luther reckoned suffering among the marks of the true church, and one of the memoranda drawn up in preparation for the Augsburg Convention similarly defines the church as the community of those "who are persecuted and martyred for the gospel's sake." . . . Discipleship means allegiance to the suffering Christ, and it is therefore not at all surprising that Christians should be called upon to suffer.*[9]

4. PASTORS ARE THE FATHERS OF THE CHURCH FAMILY (4:14-21)

After Paul's broadside of criticism in verses 8-13, he is anxious to reassure the Corinthians regarding his motive. The effect of his words might well be humiliating, but that was not their purpose. It was important for him to emphasize this because "Corinth was a city where public boasting and self-promotion had become an art form. The Corinthian people . . . lived within an honor-shame cultural orientation, where public recognition was often more important than facts and where the worst thing that could happen was for one's reputation to be publicly tarnished."[10] So Paul assures them, *I am not writing this to shame you, but to warn you, as my dear children* (v. 14). Indeed, his whole attitude to them is determined by this fact that he was their father, not their guardian. *Even though you have ten thousand guardians (paidagōgoi) in Christ, you do not have many fathers* (v. 15). Now the *paidagōgos* was not the teacher, as the anglicized form *pedagogue* would suggest. The *paidagōgos* was a slave charged with the supervision of a boy during his minority. He was responsible for the boy's dress, food, speech and manners, and would accompany him to school. He was a disciplinarian allowed to administer corporal punishment, so that he was often depicted in ancient drawings as wielding a rod (see v. 21). "But the motivation of the *paidagōgos* would be either one of paid duty or one of obedience to the instructions of the slave's master, not love for the child."[11]

Paul's claim to spiritual fatherhood is at first sight perplexing, since Jesus told us not to call anybody our father on earth because we have a Father in heaven (Mt 23:9). Of course we all have an earthly father, but Jesus was referring to having fathers in the church. So is Paul contradicting Jesus? Is he doing what Jesus told us not to do? No, he is not. Jesus was telling us not to adopt toward any Christian leader in the church, or to expect anybody to adopt toward us in our own leadership roles, the dependent relationship of children to their parents. The followers of Jesus are to grow into a healthy independence and interdependence. In other words, Jesus was forbidding that we assume the authority of a father; Paul, by contrast, is referring to a father's affection for his children. Indeed, in 1 Thessalonians 2:7 he also likens himself to a mother with her babies. It is a beautiful picture of love, self-sacrifice and gentleness.

It is because Paul can say that *in Christ Jesus I became your father through the gospel* (1 Cor 4:15), having led them to faith in Christ, and because he loves them with a father's love that he can go on: *Therefore I urge you to imitate me* (v. 16) and so "prove your parentage by your conduct."[12] He now adds another sign of his love for them. He is sending Timothy to them. Timothy is his son, as they are, and Paul is able to testify to Timothy's Christian love and faithfulness. Among other things, Timothy is faithful as a teacher. Paul is confident about this. *He will remind you of my way of life in Christ Jesus, which agrees with what I teach everywhere in every church* (v. 17). The apostle's teaching was consistent; he was not giving, nor should the Corinthians expect from him, special treatment or divergent instruction.

This emphasis on parental love and its characteristics must not be misunderstood. There is still a place for discipline in the church (as will become clear in 1 Corinthians 5 in the case of the incestuous offender), though it needs to be exercised collectively. But he hopes this will not be necessary in Corinth. For some of them *have become arrogant*, "inflated with self-importance,"[13] as if he were not coming to them (4:18). But he is intending to come very soon, God willing, and then he will discover for himself *not only how these arrogant people are talking, but what power they have* (v. 19), especially whether it is power through weakness. *For the kingdom of God is not a matter of talk but of power* (v. 20).

What then is the authentic characteristic of Christian leaders? It is not severity but gentleness. We are to be loving fathers and mothers of the church family rather than strict disciplinarians. Paul could decide to visit Corinth with an apostle's authority and challenge the arrogant. But he chooses not to—or rather, he leaves the choice to them. He concludes these chapters with a question to the Corinthians. *What do you prefer? Shall I come to you with a whip, or in love and with a gentle spirit?* (v. 21). He leaves his question unanswered. It is up to them.

CONCLUSION

Christ or Culture?

During the last thirty-five years or so I have had the privilege of traveling to many countries and observing the church and its leadership. As a result, it is my firm conviction that there is too much autocracy in the leaders of the Christian community, in defiance of the teaching of Jesus and his apostles, and not enough love and gentleness. Too many behave as if they believed not in the priesthood of all believers but in the papacy of all pastors.

Our model of leadership is often shaped more by culture than by Christ. Yet many cultural models of leadership are incompatible with the servant imagery taught and exhibited by the Lord Jesus. Nevertheless, these alien cultural models are often transplanted uncritically into the church and its hierarchy. In Africa it is the tribal chief, in Latin America the machismo (exaggerated masculinity) of the Spanish male, in South Asia the religious guru fawned on by his disciples, in East Asia the Confucian legacy of the teacher's unchallengeable authority, and in Britain the British Raj mentality—the overbearing pride associated with the period of British rule until Indian independence in 1947. It is easy for Christian leaders to assimilate one or other of these models without realizing it. But we need to determine that there is no place in the Christian community for the guru or the Confucian teacher or the African chief, for British Raj mentality or Spanish machismo. These models are not congruous with the spirit of love and gentleness.

James Stalker was a Scottish minister and author at the end of the nineteenth century. In one of his books he wrote:

> When I first was settled in a church, I discovered a thing of which no-body had told me, and which I had not anticipated, but which proved a tremendous aid in doing the work of the ministry. I fell in love with my congregation. I do not know how otherwise to express it. It was as genuine a blossom of the heart as any which I have ever experienced. It made it easy to do anything for my people.[1]

We have considered in 1 Corinthians 4 four models of ministry Paul paints of his own apostolic ministry which are also applicable to Christian leaders today, even though they are not apostles. "This is how you should regard us," Paul writes. "We are underlings of Christ, stewards of revelation, the scum of the earth and the fathers of the church family."

Further, the common denominator of all four is humility: humility before Christ, whose subordinates we are; humility before Scripture, of which we are stewards; humility before the world, whose opposition we are bound to encounter; and humility before the congregation, whose members we are to love and serve. My prayer as we come to the end of this study is that Christian leaders who peruse these pages may be characterized above all else by what the apostle Paul called "the meekness and gentleness of Christ" (2 Cor 10:1).

Notes

Chapter 1: The Ambiguity of the Church

[1]John Newton, quoted by J. C. Ryle in the chapter "Are You Regenerate?" in *Home Truths*, 9th ed. (London: Chas. J. Thynne, n.d.), pp. 94-95.

[2]Anthony Thiselton, *The First Epistle to the Corinthians,* New International Greek Testament Commentary (Grand Rapids, Mich.: Eerdmans, 2000), p. 74.

[3]John Chrysostom *Homilies on the First Epistle of St. Paul the Apostle to the Corinthians* 1.2.7.

[4]C. K. Barrett, *The First Epistle to the Corinthians*, Black's New Testament Commentaries, 2nd ed. (London: A. & C. Black, 1971), p. 46.

[5]Gordon D. Fee, *The First Epistle to the Corinthians*, New International Commentary on the New Testament (Grand Rapids, Mich.: Eerdmans, 1987), p. 61.

[6]Charles H. Hodge, *The First Epistle to the Corinthians,* 6th ed. (Edinburgh: Banner of Truth, 1959), p. 14.

Chapter 2: Power Through Weakness

[1]Gordon D. Fee, *The First Epistle to the Corinthians*, New International Commentary on the New Testament (Grand Rapids, Mich.: Eerdmans, 1987), p. 75.

[2]Archibald Robertson and Alfred Plummer, *A Critical and Exegetical Commentary on the First Epistle of St. Paul to the Corinthians*, International Critical Commentary (London: T & T Clark, 1911), p. 16.

[3]Ben Witherington III, *Conflict and Community in Corinth: A Socio-Rhetorical Commentary on 1 & 2 Corinthians* (Grand Rapids, Mich.: Eerdmans, 1995), p. 109.

[4]Fee, *First Epistle to the Corinthians*, p. 75.

[5]Cicero *In Defense of Rabirius* 5.16.

[6]*The Guardian*, August 3, 1979.

[7]Anthony Thiselton, *The First Epistle to the Corinthians,* New International Greek Testament Commentary (Grand Rapids, Mich.: Eerdmans, 2000), p. 120.

[8]See F. F. Bruce's comment on verse 26 in his *1 and 2 Corinthians*, New Century Bible (London: Marshall Morgan & Scott, 1971), p. 36.

[9]Martin Luther, quoted by Karl Barth in *The Epistle to the Romans,* trans. from the 6th ed. (London: Oxford University Press, 1933), p. 42.

[10]*China's Millions* 1, no. 5 (1875): 55.

[11]C. C. Black, quoted in Witherington, *Conflict and Community in Corinth,* p. xiii. For more material on rhetoric in the ancient world, see Donald Carson, Douglas Moo and Leon Morris, eds., *An Introduction to the New Testament* (Grand Rapids, Mich.: Zondervan, 1992), pp. 281-82; G. A. Kennedy, *The Art of Rhetoric in the Roman World 300 B.C.—300 A.D.* (Princeton, N.J.: Princeton University Press, 1972); A. Duane Litfin, *St. Paul's Theology of Proclamation: An Investigation of 1 Cor. 1—4 in the Light of Greco-Roman Rhetoric* (Cambridge: Cambridge University Press, 1994), especially pp. 296ff.; and Bruce Winter, "Rhetoric," in *Dictionary of Paul and his Letters,* ed. Gerald F. Hawthorne, Ralph P. Martin and Daniel G. Reid (Downers Grove, Ill.: InterVarsity Press, 1993), pp. 821-22.

[12]Witherington, *Conflict and Community in Corinth,* p. 40.

[13]Ibid., pp. 40-42.

[14]Ibid., p. 42.

[15]Ibid.

[16]See Thiselton, *First Epistle to the Corinthians,* pp. 14-15.

[17]Donald A. Carson, *The Cross and Christian Ministry: An Exposition of Passages from 1 Corinthians* (Grand Rapids, Mich.: Baker, 1993), p. 34.

[18]Thiselton, *First Epistle to the Corinthians,* p. 208.

[19]The exact quotation is in *The Acts of Paul and Thecla,* which may be found in E. Hennecke, *New Testament Apocrypha,* vol. 2 (London: Lutterworth, 1963), pp. 353-54.

[20]Fee, *First Epistle to the Corinthians,* p. 95.

[21]See Lewis Drummond's biography *Spurgeon: Prince of Preachers* (Grand Rapids, Mich.: Kregel, 1992), especially pp. 177, 213.

Chapter 3: Holy Spirit and Holy Scripture

[1]Gordon D. Fee, *The First Epistle to the Corinthians,* New International Commentary on the New Testament (Grand Rapids, Mich.: Eerdmans, 1987), pp. 102-5.

[2]Donald A. Carson, *The Cross and Christian Ministry: An Exposition of Passages from 1 Corinthians* (Grand Rapids, Mich.: Baker, 1993), p. 47.

[3]C. K. Barrett, *The First Epistle to the Corinthians,* Black's New Testament Commentaries, 2nd ed. (London: A. & C. Black, 1971), p. 69.

[4]F. F. Bruce, *1 and 2 Corinthians,* New Century Bible (London: Marshall Morgan & Scott, 1971), p. 38.

[5]Anthony Thiselton, *The First Epistle to the Corinthians,* New International Greek Testament Commentary (Grand Rapids, Mich.: Eerdmans, 2000), p. 257.

[6]Quoted by J. C. Ryle in *Christian Leaders of England in the Eighteenth Century* (London: Chas. J. Thynne, n.d.), p. 111.

Chapter 4: The Church and the Trinity

[1]Donald A. Carson, *The Cross and Christian Ministry: An Exposition of Passages from 1 Corinthians* (Grand Rapids, Mich.: Baker, 1993), pp. 71, 75.

[2]I owe this information to Keith Buckler, who was kind enough to write to me during the Keswick Convention in July 2001.

[3]C. K. Barrett, *The First Epistle to the Corinthians,* Black's New Testament Commentaries, 2nd ed. (London: A. & C. Black, 1971), p. 80.

[4]Charles H. Hodge, *The First Epistle to the Corinthians,* 6th ed. (Edinburgh: Banner of Truth, 1959), p. 49.

[5]Gordon D. Fee, *The First Epistle to the Corinthians,* New International Commentary on the New Testament (Grand Rapids, Mich.: Eerdmans, 1987), p. 125.

[6]J. B. Lightfoot, *Notes on Epistles of St. Paul* (London: Macmillan, 1895), p. 187.

[7]Barrett, *First Epistle to the Corinthians,* p. 87.

[8]Thomas Charles Edwards, *A Commentary on the First Epistle to the Corinthians* (London: Hamilton, Adams, 1885), p. 81.

Chapter 5: Models of Ministry

[1]Mark Twain, *The Adventures of Huckleberry Finn* (London: Pan Books, 1968), p. 347.

[2]George Carey, *Canterbury Letters to the Future* (London: Kingsway, 1998), p. 121.

[3]Archibald Robertson and Alfred Plummer, *A Critical and Exegetical Commentary on the First Epistle of St. Paul to the Corinthians,* International Critical Commentary (London: T & T Clark, 1911), p. 74.

[4]Anthony Thiselton, *The First Epistle to the Corinthians,* New International Greek Testament Commentary (Grand Rapids, Mich.: Eerdmans, 2000), p. 335.

[5]Robertson and Plummer, *Critical and Exegetical Commentary,* p. 81.

[6]F. D. Coggan, *Stewards of Grace* (London: Hodder & Stoughton, 1958), pp. 46, 48.

[7]Robertson and Plummer, *Critical and Exegetical Commentary,* p. 84. Cf. C. K. Barrett, *The First Epistle to the Corinthians,* Black's New Testament Commentaries, 2nd ed. (London: A. & C. Black, 1971), p. 109.

[8]G. G. Findlay, *St. Paul's First Epistle to the Corinthians,* Expositor's Greek Testament, 2nd ed., vol. 2 (London: Hodder & Stoughton, 1901), p. 803.

[9]Dietrich Bonhoeffer, *The Cost of Discipleship* (London: SCM Press, 1959), p. 74.

[10]Ben Witherington III, *Conflict and Community in Corinth: A Socio-Rhetorical Commentary on 1 & 2 Corinthians* (Grand Rapids, Mich.: Eerdmans, 1995), p. 8.

[11]Thiselton, *First Epistle to the Corinthians*, p. 370.

[12]Robertson and Plummer, *Critical and Exegetical Commentary*, p. 90.

[13]Thiselton, *First Epistle to the Corinthians*, p. 376.

Conclusion: Christ or Culture?

[1]James Stalker, *The Preacher and His Models* (London: Hodder & Stoughton, 1891), p. 231.

Study Guide

The aim of this study guide is to help you get to the heart of what John Stott has written and to challenge you to apply what you learn to your own life. The questions have been designed for use both by individuals and also by small groups of Christians meeting, perhaps for an hour or two each week, to study, discuss and pray together.

The guide provides material for each of the five chapters and the conclusion of the book. When used by a group with limited time, the leader should decide beforehand which questions are most appropriate for the group to discuss during the meeting. The rest could perhaps be left for group members to work through by themselves or in smaller groups during the week.

In order to be able to contribute fully and learn from the group meetings, each member of the group needs to read through the chapter or chapters under discussion.

It is important not to let these studies become merely academic exercises. Guard against this by making time to think through and discuss how what you discover works out in practice for you. Make sure you begin and end each study with a time of focusing on God in praise and prayer. Ask the Holy Spirit to speak to you through your discussion together.

Theme 1: The Ambiguity of the Church (1 Corinthians 1:1-17)
1. What is the "paradox at the heart of the church" (p. 17)? Can you illustrate this from your own experience?
2. How does Stott justify what he says about the uniqueness of the authority and ministry of the New Testament apostles? Why is this such an important issue today? (See pp. 18-19.)
3. As you reflect on your own attitude to the New Testament, would you say that you are "humbly under its authority" (pp. 19-20)? What does this mean in practice?
4. What is so "extraordinary" (pp. 20-21) about the existence of the church in Corinth?
5. In what ways is the "ambiguity of the church" (pp. 21-22) indicated by what Paul

says in verse 2? Can you think of any dangers that might result from abandoning either side of this tension?

6. What do we know about Paul's relationship with the church at Corinth? Why is it important to bear this in mind when reading what he writes to them? (See p. 22.)

7. How does Paul emphasize the worldwide scope of the Christian community? Why is this important? How is it expressed in the church to which you belong? (See p. 23.)

8. Do you believe that "each local church . . . may expect to be given collectively all the gifts it needs" (p. 24)? How does this apply in your situation?

9. As we look around at the obvious flaws in the church as we know it, how can we have any confidence that it will one day be perfect? (See pp. 24-25.)

10. Why is the unity of the church so important to Paul? (See pp. 25-26.) Is it as important to you?

11. Is there anyone in the church whom you find it difficult to regard as a brother or sister? What do you think Paul would say to you?

12. From what Paul writes here, can we identify any of the causes of disunity in the church at Corinth? (See pp. 26-27.)

13. In what way were the Corinthians "effectively insulting Christ" (pp. 27-28) by their attitudes?

14. What can we learn from the way Paul "lingers on the topic of baptism" (pp. 28-29) in verses 14-17?

15. Why is Paul so insistent that his communication of the gospel of Christ was *not with words of human wisdom* (v. 17; p. 29)?

16. Faced with the ambiguity of the church, do you tend toward being a perfectionist or a defeatist (p. 30)? In what ways do you experience "the painful tension between the 'already' and the 'not yet'" (p. 30)?

Theme 2: Power Through Weakness (1 Corinthians 1:18—2:5)

1. In what ways does a hunger for power reveal itself in the church to which you belong? (See pp. 35-36.)

2. What do people mean when they ask God to give them "power"? How does this match up to what the New Testament tells us the Holy Spirit's power is for? (See pp. 36-38.)

3. In what ways does the church at Corinth demonstrate the principle of God's power working best through weakness? (See pp. 44-45.)

4 What exactly is "the message of the cross" (pp. 39-40)? Why does it provoke such diametrically opposed reactions?

5. What threefold division of humanity does Paul express here? (See pp. 40-41.)

How do you think this is reflected in today's world? Into which erroneous path are you more likely to stray? Why?

6. Why is the cross "an absolute stumbling block" to those who worship power (pp. 41-42)? How does Stott highlight the main way in which people express this today? (See pp. 42-43.)

7. Why is the message of the cross so foolish to people? (See p. 43.) What experience have you had of this?

8. In what ways does the cross display the power and wisdom of God? (See p. 43.)

9. Why does God choose "foolish, weak and lowly people" (p. 44)? Are you content to be labeled in this way?

10. What "three great blessings we enjoy in Christ" (p. 44) does Paul identify here? What do they mean to you?

11. If God's saving power is exhibited in human weakness, where does that leave those who are "clever, wealthy, influential or socially prominent" (pp. 45-46)?

12. If you had met Paul, do you think he would have struck you as being "weak and feeble" (pp. 46-47)? What does he mean?

13. What lessons are there here for the preachers of today? (See p. 48.)

14. What comes to mind when you come across the phrase *a demonstration of the Spirit's power* (2:4; p. 49)? What does Paul mean by it?

15. What illustrations of the "'power through weakness' principle" (pp. 50-51) can you think of? How might it apply to you, and how might you more effectively put it into practice?

Theme 3: Holy Spirit and Holy Scripture (1 Corinthians 2:6-16)

1. What does Paul mean by *a message of wisdom among the mature* (2:6; pp. 57-59)? Is he referring to first-class and second-class Christians?

2. Given that Paul is not abandoning wisdom altogether, how does he qualify what he means by it? (See p. 58.)

3. What exactly is "God's wisdom for the mature" (p. 58)? How does this point to "a legitimate distinction between evangelism and Christian nurture" (p. 59)?

4. How does Paul underline "the necessity of revelation" (pp. 59-60) here? According to what he says here, how exactly does God reveal himself to us? (See p. 61.)

5. What are the Holy Spirit's "unique qualifications" (p. 62) when it comes to revealing God to us? What does this tell us about who the Holy Spirit is? (See pp. 62-63.)

6. What are the "two separate but related gifts" (p. 64) that the apostles received from God? How is Paul such a good example of this? (See p. 64.)

7. How does the Spirit's activity in revealing truth to the apostles filter through to us

today? (See p. 65.)

8. In what ways is the phrase "verbal inspiration" (pp. 66-67) sometimes misunderstood? What does it actually mean?

9. Why are some Christians today perhaps "embarrassed by, or afraid of, this traditional Christian belief" (pp. 67-68)? How about you?

10. What distinction needs to be made between the Holy Spirit's work of revelation and inspiration on the one hand, and his work of illumination on the other? Why is this so important? (See pp. 68-69.)

11. If, as Paul says, *we have the mind of Christ* (2:16), why do Christians disagree? What can we do to put this right? (See pp. 71-72.)

12. What are the practical consequences for you of the assertion that "the Word and the Spirit belong to each other" (pp. 73-74)?

Theme 4: The Church and the Trinity (1 Corinthians 3)

1. What is the "connecting link" between 1 Corinthians 2 and 3? Why is the NIV translation "unfortunate" (p. 79) here?

2. What has persuaded Paul that his readers are carnal and infantile rather than spiritual and mature? (See p. 80.) What do you think he would make of your church?

3. What exactly is the difference between spiritual solid food and spiritual milk? (See pp. 80-81.) How does this apply in practice?

4. What then is "Paul's threefold indictment of the Corinthian Christians" (p. 82)? To what can their failures be attributed?

5. What images of the church does Paul develop here? (See pp. 82-83.)

6. What particular lesson does the metaphor of the field have for us? (See pp. 83-86.)

7. In light of what Paul says here, does your church have a problem with the way it views its leaders?

8. What does Paul say in 3:8-9 that "demonstrates the stupidity of the Corinthians' behavior" (p. 85)?

9. What further point is made by the metaphor of the building? (See pp. 86-87.) How does this apply to you?

10. What do *gold, silver, costly stones* and *wood, hay or straw* (3:12) represent in the life of the church? In what way is there a "solemn warning here to all Christian teachers" (p. 88)?

11. What further point does Paul make through his picture of the church as God's temple? (See pp. 89-91.)

12. What is the "climax of the passage" (p. 92) here? How might this apply in your situation?

13. In what ways is "who belongs to whom in the church . . . still a vital issue today" (pp. 92-93)?

14. Do you think the leaders in your church tend to think of the congregation as "their" people? (See p. 93.) To what does this lead?

Theme 5: Models of Ministry (1 Corinthians 4)

1. What do you think the church's clergy are for? Do you tend toward clericalism or anticlericalism? Why?

2. What "four essentials of authentic pastoral ministry" (p. 100) does Paul set out here?

3. What does John Stott declare to be "fundamental to all Christian leadership and ministry" (p. 103)? In what ways is this both comforting and challenging? (See pp. 101-3.)

4. In what sense are today's Christian pastors "stewards of God's revelation" (pp. 103-4)? What are the "three important facts" (p. 104) that follow from this?

5. What are the "three vivid metaphors" (p. 105) that Paul uses in 4:8-13 to illustrate the nature of true Christian leadership? (See pp. 105-7.) How does what he says apply to you?

6. If you are a Christian leader, what experience have you had of the temptation to be popular at the expense of being faithful? (See p. 108.) How do you handle this?

7. What is it about the gospel that arouses people's opposition? (See pp. 108-9.) Does it do this when you preach or explain it? Why?

8. What is "at first sight perplexing" (p. 110) about Paul's claim to spiritual fatherhood? What point is he seeking to get across?

9. In your experience, do church leaders display paternal authority or paternal affection? Why is this distinction so crucial? (See pp. 110-11.)

Conclusion: Christ or Culture?

1. Do you share Stott's "firm conviction that there is too much autocracy in the leaders of the Christian community" (p. 113)? What can you do about this problem?

2. What is the "common denominator" (p. 114) of all four models of ministry that Paul sets out here? What is its source?